What knitters say about the e-Book of The Mermaid Shawl & other Beauties:

Worth every cent, in my opinion. This is one I will read and re-read. - MMario on Knitter's Review *and*

Small but mighty. I think her comments on design, and design choices are extremely insightful; there is a bonus of a short story; and there is not only multiple designs but coaching on designing your own variations. Looking forward to the sequels - if they are half as informative as "Mermaid" they will be well worth the price! - MMario on Ravelry.com

Just got my hands on your e-book "Mermaid Shawls", and am absolutely delighted! Thanks for all the tips, suggestions ~ and heart ~ that are in the book. It is wonderful! - KathyO in Ferndale, WA

I just bought your book, after looking at the inside. It is just what I have been looking for. Your illustrations and commentary have eased my fear of starting a shawl. - Margaret in Canada

I just bought and downloaded the book and have completely and absolutely fallen in love with it. We seem to have a similarity in the way we think about knitting and it makes the book an even greater joy for me to read. Right now I'm in the middle of reading it and am pretty much useless to the rest of the world as nothing else gets through. Thank you so much for writing the book and offering it for sale, it's a real joy. - Ella on Ravelry.com

I just bought a copy and it is printing as we speak! Gorgeous!! I cannot wait! And I especially love that the shawls look substantial - I am not sold on cobweb-weight scarfs/stoles/shawls. - Lyeth on Ravelry.com

In **The Mermaid Shawl & other Beauties: Shawls, Cocoons & Wraps** you will find:

- Layouts for three shawl styles with directions for making many variations
- Detailed instruction for a dozen projects
- Directions for transforming a rectangular shawl into a cocoon
- A chapter on knitting on the bias
- Dozens of photographs and charts for lace patterns
- Commentary on buying yarn, choosing needles, following charts and more
- A seductive short story based on the signature shawl
- Advice and encouragement for making a masterpiece of your own!

The Mermaid
Shawl & other Beauties

SHAWLS, COCOONS & WRAPS

KATHLEEN VALENTINE

Parlez-Moi Press

ISBN: 0-9785940-2-9

ISBN-13: 978-0-9785940-2-2

www.MermaidShawl.com
www.ParlezMoiPress.com
www.KathleenValentine.com
www.ParlezMoiBlog.blogspot.com

Photography by Kathleen Valentine
Models: Jane Daniel, Clare Higgins, Constance Rohrbough
Photographed in Gloucester, Massachusetts.

Exceptions:
Rebecca's Shawl (back cover, frontispiece, page 15) photography by David Montgomery
Model: Rebecca Reynolds
Photographed at Montgomery's Boatyard, Gloucester

Emily's Shawl (front cover, back cover, page 20) photography by Paula Ryan
Model: Emily Beimel
Photographed in Manhattan Beach, California

Beth's Shawl (back cover, pages viii, 21) photography by Casimir J. Pelligrini
Model: Beth Valentine Pelligrini
Photographed in Pittsburgh, Pennsylvania

Additional scenic photography by Jay Albert
www.CapeAnnImages.blogspot.com

Book design by Valentine-Design.com

Parlez-Moi Press
Gloucester, Massachusetts

In loving memory
of Gram, Christine Werner, who taught me to crochet, sew, quilt, and embroider but who never learned to knit
and
of Sister Imelda, O.S.B. who taught me the value of draftsmanship
"Ora et labora"

TABLE OF CONTENTS

A Word to Beginners: Fear Not!

If you are a novice knitter who looks at the garments in this book and thinks "Oh, I could never..." STOP RIGHT THERE! Yes, you can. If you can knit and purl, and can learn to knit 2 stitches together, you can make all of the Knitting-on-the Bias designs. If you can then learn to make yarn overs (YO) and can knit 2 stitches together, you can make the Scrap Bag Stole (above), the Silk Roving Wrap, and the Gypsy Shawl . Once you have done any of those you can use the very same techniques to make Beth's Shawl.

After that you will be a lace knitter and there will be no stopping you!

LOOK, MA, I'M KNITTING!

Look, Ma, I'm Knitting!

For years friends have been urging me to do something with my Lace knitting designs—teach, write, publish, whatever. I always resisted for three reasons.

1. I am a large-sized woman and I could never figure out how to scale the things I make for myself down for other sizes. I tend to be a one-of-a-kind knitter and rarely want to make the same thing twice.
2. I knit weird. I hold my yarn in my left hand, which is popular in Europe but not here, and that makes it difficult to teach people because they don't understand what I am doing.
3. I am incapable of following instructions. I make things up as I go along with the assistance of charts in various knitting books but reading line-by-line instructions makes me crazy.

However, all that being said, I've decided to write this book anyway and I am giving this introduction as fair warning. If you are a knitter who likes to follow instructions to the letter, this is not the book for you. If you are a knitter who is uncomfortable with trial and error, this is not the book for you. And if you are a knitter who wants things to be exact and precise, this is not the book for you. But, if you are a knitter who has made a few garments, is comfortable with your needles and your materials, and who is interested in developing skills that will expand your range as a knitter, this book might be just what you need.

This is my theory, if I tell you how I approach knitting including choosing fiber, deciding how to use it, swatching (I know, I know, you hate that word), how I plan a garment and adjust my knitting as I proceed, how I use charted stitch patterns by knitters more accomplished than I am, and how I figure the size of my finished piece, you then can do the same things for your own garments.

My Knitting Philosophy

I believe that knitting should be both creative and meditative. I believe it should nurture creativity and provide serenity. I think that time spent with the needle should be relaxing and satisfying as we see Lace tumbling down from our needles. I believe each creation should be unique to its creator.

In this book I hope to give you the inspiration to take the diagrams for the various projects and use them to create unique works or art that are yours alone. I hope you will experiment with different fibers and different size needles and play with color. But most of all I hope you will begin combining different types of Lace Patterns—the knitting world is full of them—in your own combinations to make your own creations. If there are 100 Lace Patterns in a book and one of my diagrams calls for 3 of them that means that over 970,000 completely unique shawls could be made from that one diagram—and that doesn't count differences of color, texture, fiber, and size.

I want every garment you knit to be as unique and beautiful as the knitter who knitted it.

MY KNITTING AUTOBIOGRAPHY

Actually, it was my brother Wayne who taught me to knit. We were kids and he had learned from one of the nuns at school. She knit on the playground and he, being the curious kid he was, watched her instead of playing. She brought him a pair of needles and some yarn and taught him to knit. He brought it home and showed me. Thus began a life-long love for me. I don't know if Wayne still remembers how to knit but I'm sure he could pick it up quickly.

I subsequently knew a couple of knitting nuns during my twelve years in Catholic school and they helped me learn a few more advanced things like purling and increasing and decreasing. For years all I could do was make scarves—long, colorful scarves that I made in many colors and from many yarns. My Grandmother Werner sewed and crocheted but there were no other knitters in my life so I bought a book (I still have it), **A Treasury of Aran Knitting Patterns**, and taught myself to make Aran sweaters. Within a few years everyone in my life had one of my Aran sweaters, whether they wanted one or not.

I moved to New England in 1988 and put my knitting to good use. I placed an ad in the Swop column of Yankee Magazine and offered to knit an Aran style sweater in "your choice of color and size" in exchange for two or three nights stay in an inn or bed and breakfast along the coast. This turned into quite an adventure. For several years I knitted like crazy while traveling from Wellfleet and Nantucket to Mount Dessert Island in Maine. Usually the rooms I stayed in were available in the off-season so I would pack my car or board a ferry with a backpack full of yarn and needles for the next project. Bundled in homemade sweaters, I'd hike up to headlands overlooking the Atlantic Ocean or sit by fireplaces in small pubs and work on the sweater for my next hosts while drinking in my surroundings (and a little wine, too). Those knitting adventures served two purposes. Not only did I get to stay in places I could not afford, but it fed my writer's passion for watching people and experiencing new places.

Living in New England opened a whole new world of knitting excitement for me. I started going to knitting workshops but, much to my chagrin, I learned I had a handicap---I knit holding my yarn in my left hand, not my right, like most knitters. I had no difficulty adapting when learning new stitches and patterns but when I tried to show a technique to another knitter they got confused. I had also discovered that I could not follow written directions. I had no trouble when patterns were charted but line-by-line instructions confused me terribly. Also, because I am a large-sized woman, I found that the directions given for most patterns I liked were too small for me. Thus began a long period of experimentation.

One winter I attended a workshop with Kaffe Fassett in Lexington. The way he used yarn and color and patterns absolutely blew my mind. I had never seen anything like it. I was an art major in college and was working as a graphic designer. Suddenly the idea of using fibers, patterns and color, to create works of art became a consuming passion. I bought his Glorious Knits and drove to Uxbridge, Massachusetts where Ironstone Yarns had

an outlet store and, for a pittance, bought a huge bag of odds and ends of mohair yarn in dozens of colors. I knit out of that bag for years. I made my version of a Fassett knit out of pastel mohair and I also acquired a book that would prove to be transformative to my knitting, Knitting with Mohair by Melinda Coss and Debby Robinson. In that book I saw my first "picture" sweater (the Carmen Miranda Sweater). Plus they charted their patterns in color. Using the techniques I learned in that book I made my first picture sweater out of Ballybrae wool (closeup on previous page, back below). I couldn't stop knitting.

For years I had flirted with the idea of trying to knit lace. I had taken Barbara Walker's books out of the library many times but got frustrated trying to follow the written directions. I'm a highly visual person and written directions just baffled me. Then one day I picked up Marianne Kinzel's Second Book of Lace Knitting and everything changed. She had charts! I could follow charts! What a joy. I had learned to adapt to knitting with yarn in my left hand. I'd learned how to adjust patterns to my size. Now, suddenly, I could understand lace knitting patterns! I was in love.

Since that day, knitting lace has become my favorite form of knitting. As I made scarves and shawls and cocoons and wraps I discovered that knitting lace gave me a sense of satisfaction that I never found in any other form of knitting.

The results are in this book.

Previous page, closeup of the front of my Cape Ann sweater that I charted on graph paper I made on my computer (to approximate stitch proportions) and knit out of Ballybrae wool. The front features a ship's figurehead passing the twin stone lighthouses on Thacher's Island in Rockport, MA. with cresting waves and a moon emerging from the clouds. The borders are rows of seagulls.

This page, the back of that sweater which features a whale's tail and the Cape Ann Lighthouse. Photographed at Flatrock off of Eden Road overlooking the real Cape Ann Lighthouse. (Photos by Trudi Forti, 1994)

MY PROCESS

Don't you hate people who say things like, "There are two kinds of people in the world, those who..." Yeah, they drive me nuts, too. But there are two kinds of knitters in the world, those who love to do the preparation work before starting to knit and those who don't. I am in the first group. I love to experiment with the yarn I am about to use, to knit little swatches on different sized needles, and to experiment with interesting stitches or pair one yarn with another just to see what sort of effect I can get. If you are the sort of knitter who just wants to get started knitting, well, you might not be too happy with what I am about to tell you: You have to do some prep work if you want to knit the designs in this book. There's a reason for this: I want you to work with fibers you love, not the fibers someone tells you to use. And I want you to play with lace patterns, not just the ones I use. I want your knitting to be fun and creative.

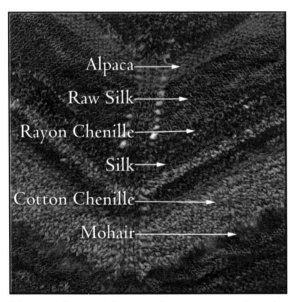

This swatch shows six different fibers knit on the same needles in the same pattern. It gives a sense of what works and what does not.

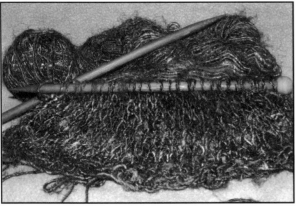

This is the Himalayan Recycled Silk used in the Gypsy Shawl. It took quite a few swatches to get the needle size right.

About Fiber

I love fiber, the softer the better. For years I worked with whatever I could afford but these days if I am going to make something I want it to be of the loveliest fiber I can find. I collect yarn and, like many knitters, have quite a stash. Probably my favorite fiber to knit with is Pima Cotton. It is deliciously soft, washes well, wears well, and comes in both smooth and fuzzy yarns. I also love working with silk of all kinds, cashmere when I can get it at a good price, and alpaca. Wool, especially Merino wool, can be lovely, too. One of the wonderful things about being a knitter today is that there are so many options that didn't exist a generation ago.

The Gypsy Shawl in this book is knit entirely of Himalayan Recycled Silk. Recycled sari silk began in the sari manufacturing regions of Asia. Women who worked in the mills carried home scraps of the leftover fabric and spun the scraps into yarns that they used to knit hats and jackets for their children. Eventually these yarns arrived in the west and passion for recycled sari silk spread like wildfire among western knitters. Today much of the sari silk comes from used saris that have been cleaned and shredded for spinning.

One of the marvelous things that the current knitting trend has done is provide a much needed economic resource for spinners around the world. It makes me very happy to know that knitters are supporting entire villages in the Himalayas and the Andes, in Wales and in Haiti, with their passion for unique and wonderful yarns. Whenever possible I try to buy from vendors who buy their yarns from native spinners.

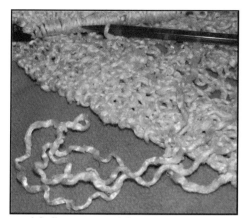

Recycled silk roving unraveled from a sweater purchased for $5 in a thrift store.

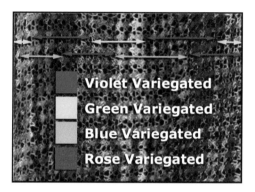

Four variegated lace-weight yarns were used for the Striped Shawl working with 2 held together. This chart shows how the four different shades were overlapped to create a softer color change effect. In the sample below two strands of laceweight wool in slightly different shades are being worked together.

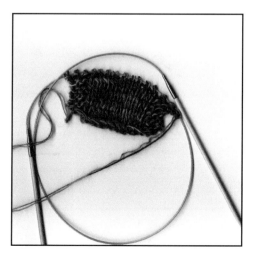

Recycled yarn doesn't have to be limited to that which comes from other countries. There are a number of eBay vendors who purchase cashmere, silk and wool sweaters in thrift stores, clean them and then unravel and wind the yarns for reuse. The Silk Roving Wrap was made from a loose-knit pure silk sweater purchased in a thrift store for $5 (left). As I took it apart I realized that the fiber had not been spun, it was soft, lustrous and very strong. The sweater had a few damaged spots but it was easy to cut those out. It took a while to unravel the yarn but is well worth it for the beautiful wrap it made.

When you consider the hours that go into knitting it is best to work with something that feels lovely in your hands, and has the ability to take your breath away when the piece is worn.

Swatch What You are Doing

I love making swatches. In my knitting youth I often plunged into projects before I really gave them adequate preparation and then tried to compensate for that by fudging as I went along. This resulted in some truly ugly items. Maybe things seem less urgent as I age but I genuinely love taking my time and testing things out before I begin a project. There is something pleasantly leisurely and undemanding about it. I don't feel compelled to get it right because I probably will just rip it out anyway. It gives me the opportunity to appreciate the fiber and let it tell me what it wants to be. I'm a great believer in letting your fiber speak to you.

You have to swatch to get a sense of how various yarns will knit up on different size needles. I usually start by casting on thirty stitches and knitting 30 rows. Then I measure and make note of the stitches per inch. I tend to measure a four inch square. That gives better accuracy.

I also try several size needles until I am happy with the density and drape of the knitted piece. If the needles are too small for your yarn, the fabric will be tight and "crowded" looking. If the needles are too large, the fabric will look sloppy and your beautifully knit lace won't show to best advantage. Take the time and try a few swatches until you find the one that says "yes!" to you.

Another reason to swatch is to teach yourself new patterns before you commit to an entire garment, or section of a garment in that pattern. It is a very individual thing but some lace patterns are just plain disagreeable to knit. They may be beautiful but if you are annoyed by the process, you won't enjoy your knitting. Sometimes a pattern that aggravates you is tolerable in small amounts—a narrow panel on either side of a stole, but would make you crazy if the entire piece was composed of it. As you can see in the swatches pictured here you learn a lot by swatching.

One of the most important lessons you will learn is that the smoother the yarn, the more precise your knitting needs to be. When you are first starting out in lace knitting it might not be a bad idea to knit with yarns

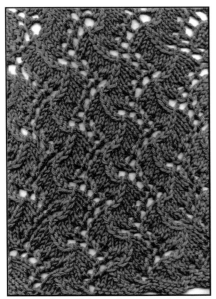

This stitch is called Traveling Vine and is shown here knit in a soft, sport-weight alpaca/silk blend. It is not an easy pattern to master but, with the help of stitch markers, the scarf was completed.

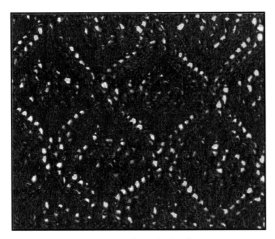

The pattern above is Rose Trellis, a lovely all-over pattern that is not as complicated as it looks. It is shown knit in a wool/angora blend which hides my many mistakes but still gives a lovely look. Below is a pattern sometimes called Shooting Star or Frost Flowers. It is knit in a smooth Pima cotton which gives excellent stitch definition, so master the pattern first!

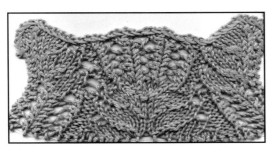

that are more textured or fuzzy. Mistakes are less obvious. As you increase in skill you will find the smoother yarns that provide greater stitch definition to be more appealing.

Finally, swatching can be a fun way to try using different yarns together. One of my favorite things is to buy a variety of laceweight yarns in different colors and then hold 2 or 3 or even 4 of them together as I knit breaking off one color and adding a new color at random intervals. That way the colors blend softly together instead of one shade abruptly ending and a new shade beginning. The Shimmer Shawl on page 31 is knit this way.

Laying Out Your Design

In each of the four sections of this book—triangle shawl, rectangle shawl and rectangle stole, and cocoon—there is a diagram in a box labeled The Basics. When I showed these drawings to my friend Maureen she got very excited because she is not a knitter, she prefers crochet. "I could use these charts and a book of crochet lace patterns to make these designs," she said. I see no reason why they could not be used by those who crochet. I often crochet the edges on my shawls. The Black Cashmere Cocoon is finished with crocheted lace.

The proportions on each of these diagrams can change in any dimension you like. Once you master the basic concepts you can adjust yarn weight, needle size, and repeat rows to make your creations as large or as small as you like. The original Mermaid Shawl in aqua Suri alpaca measures 82"x 42", a very luxurious wrap even for someone my size. When I made the second version I used a worsted weight viscose/angora yarn on size nine needles and it turned out much smaller which was good because it was a gift for my friend Rebecca who is petite.

What I hope you will do is try a few of the pieces in this book and, when you have learned the method, use that to experiment with different lace patterns and stitches to make each piece an original work of your art.

Lace Patterns

Where to begin? There are endless lace patterns some of which are exquisitely simple and others that require more discipline than I have. The lace in the Shimmer Shawl is a very simple, easily learned stitch. If you are new to lace knitting that is an excellent first project.

I collect patterns for knitted lace. I own all of the Barbara Walker and Marianne Kinzel books and a variety of other vintage lace books. I cut out pages from knitting magazines and surf the 'Net for new patterns I have never seen. One thing that I always do is count

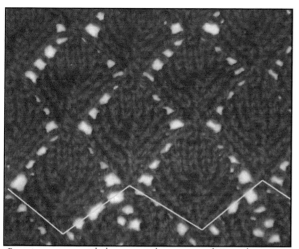

By using patterns with the same stitch repeat, two different lace patterns can "fit" together almost seamlessly for a beautiful effect.

how many stitches each pattern repeats over and I sort them accordingly. That way when I am working on a design I can pick out all my patterns with a particular repeat—12, 18, 24—and use them together. This means one pattern flows seamlessly into the next. More about this in the various chapters. Over the years I have developed a fondness for certain stitches. Old Shale, Horseshoe Lace, and Falling Leaves are three of my favorites. I use them all the time and they always look beautiful.

I suggest you begin to collect lace patterns that catch your eye. Knit a swatch to see how you like working that pattern. I keep mine in kitchen plastic bags with zipper tops. I often staple the knitted swatch to the instructions.

Now, on to the shawls.

Stitch Legend	
	Knit (blank)
—	Purl
O	Yarn Over
/	LSK2tog
\	RSK2tog
△	Slip1K2togPSSO
◁	LSK3tog
▷	RSK3tog

This beautiful fingering weight cashmere in a natural heather was great for practicing a new lace pattern. The fiber doesn't really show off the beauty of the pattern but it was good prctice and made a lovely, soft, lacy scarf.

The first Mermaid Shawl made of
Suri alpaca knit on #10 needles

The Shawl of Falling Leaves and Shooting Stars
made of Andean wool knit on #7 needles

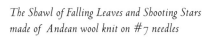

The Gypsy Shawl made of
100% recycled Himalayan silk
knit on #10 needles

THE MERMAID SHAWL
& TWO VARIATIONS

When I made my first Mermaid Shawl I had no idea it would be as lovely and as popular as it is. At the time, I was working on my first novel, The Old Mermaid's Tale. *In the story, Clair, the heroine, has dreams in which she is a mermaid. I had purchased a bag of Suri alpaca in a color called Ocean that I loved. As I tried to imagine what I could do with it, visions of Clair in her mermaid dreams haunted me. I knew I wanted a center-seamed, triangular shawl because I find them the most "snuggly" to wear. I got out my books of knitted lace patterns and one of the first patterns I turned to was called "Mermaid Lace". I then found patterns that made me think of fins and of waves, and thus the Mermaid Shawl was born. Later, I wrote a short story imagining the origins of such a shawl. I've included that story at the end of this chapter.*

Triangle shawls have been around since the beginning. It is a convenient shape because it can be crisscrossed in front and tied in back to keep the wearer warm while working. Triangle shawls with a center-seam down the back seem to drape better than those knit as a straight triangle. The first one I made was in Garter Stitch and I wore it all the time it was that cozy. Lisa's Shawl was the second center-seamed triangle shawl I made. The method is easy. you start with just a few stitches at the top center-back, knit outward and down, adding 4 stitches per row on the right side (RS).

For Lisa's Shawl I was working with a strand of silk noil in a medium green and a strand of rayon chennile in a slightly deeper green. As you can see in the photographs the pattern consisted of two sections of Stockinette Stitch divided by a single row of Eyelette Lace. In the third section there are 2 inches of Stockinette, 2 inches of Little Leaf Lace (see chart on page 31), then 2 more inches of Stockinette and a third row of Eyelette. The final section begins with Stockinette Stitch, six rows of an Eyelette knit at intervals along the length of the shawl and then seven pattern repeats of Old Shale (see chart on page 13). Finally 4 rows of Garter Stitch and the shawl is bound off, being careful to do so very loosely.

The center back seam is consistent for the entire length, YO, K1, YO on the RS and P3 on the WS.

This shawl was an experiment that worked up rather prettily. From a purely aesthetic perspective it is generally wisest to use smaller lace patterns toward the top of the shawl (in the beginning) and work larger, lacier patterns as your shawl becomes wider and longer. This accomplishes two things—the look will generally be more pleasing and the more open and lacy patterns will be toward the bottom where there is less weight. If you are working with a heavier fiber like silk or rayon this is an advantage.

Learning to add pattern repeats as the shawl grows wider can take a little time and experimentation. I

Lisa's Shawl, the second center-seamed triangle shawl I ever made in silk noil and rayon chenille knit on #8 needles

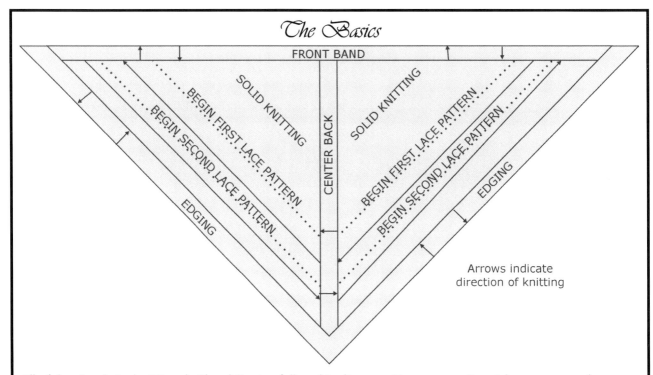

The Basics

FRONT BAND

SOLID KNITTING

SOLID KNITTING

BEGIN FIRST LACE PATTERN

BEGIN FIRST LACE PATTERN

BEGIN SECOND LACE PATTERN

BEGIN SECOND LACE PATTERN

CENTER BACK

EDGING

EDGING

Arrows indicate
direction of knitting

All of the shawls in the Triangle Shawl Section follow this diagram. You can use 2 or 3 lace patterns plus a lace Edging in addition to the solid parts of the shawl, but feel free to experiment. The Front Band and Center Back are a basic 1 x1 Rib Stitch (k1, p1). The Solid Knitting area is basic Stockinette Stitch (k on RS, p on WS). The First and Second Lace Patterns vary. So does the Edging. The Gypsy Shawl does not have Edging.

suggest using stitch markers (as shown in Figures 5, 6, 7) to help guide you. As your lace patterns become wider and more intricate you will have to make decisions about when to start another pattern repeat. Do not be intimidated by this. It is perfectly acceptable to just work in a plain pattern until you have enough stitches for another repeat of your pattern. In many ways this becomes something of a game with yourself. Don't worry about making a mistake. It will be all right.

The Mermaid Shawl

The original (pale green) Mermaid Shawl was worked in Suri alpaca on #10 needles. Eight-143-yard skeins were used, totalling 1144 yards. The second one, which was knit specifically for the Mermaid Shawl Knit-A-Long on my blog begun on Groundhog's Day in 2006, was knit in a smooth fiber to better show the workmanship. The yarn was a viscose/angora blend in pale gray. This was worked on #9 needles because, when I swatched it on #10 it looked too loose for my taste. The alpaca on #10 needles swatched to 7 stitches per 2 inches. The

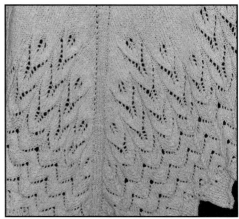

Closeup of the second Mermaid Shawl knit from viscose/angora in a color called Dove. The stitch definition is much more percise than in the original shawl and the drape is excllent.

final shawl measures 84" across and 42" down the back. The viscose knit to 7.5 stitches per 2 inches. The final shawl was approximately 72" by 36" which was perfect for its new owner.

Figure 1 - Cast on 7 and work in rib stitch according to directions.

Figure 2 - Pick up 9 stitches on one side.

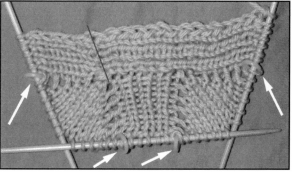

Figure 3 - Pick up 7 stitches from beginning.

Figure 4 (below) - Arrows indicate placement of markers. Pink line shows where first row is picked up and added to marker.

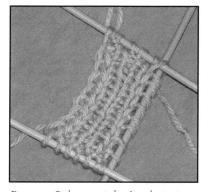

Part One - A Tricky Beginning

You will need a set of four double-pointed needles in the needle size you have chosen and a 24" (or greater) circular needle the same size. Four stitch markers and a few inches of waste yarn.

Step 1 - Cast On:
Begin knitting with 2 double-pointed needles. Using the invisible cast-on with the waste yarn (Figure 1, in gray), cast on seven stitches. Work as follows:
RS (right side): P1 (K1, P1) 3x
WS (wrong side): K1 (P1, K1) 3x
Repeat until you have worked a total of 18 rows or the number of rows you need to pick up 9 stitches along length. End on a RS row. This is the beginning of the shawl at the center top.

Step 2 - Pick Up Two Sides:
With a second double-pointed needle pick up 9 stitches along the side of the knitted piece at the end of the row you have just knit, as shown in Figure 2. Then carefully remove the waste yarn and pick up the first seven stitches with a third double-pointed. Because you are going to work in the opposite direction, the stitches will be reversed from the opposite side of the ribbing (Figure 3), therefore make 1 Purl-wise stitch at the beginning of the row.

Step 3 - Begin Increase Pattern:
With the piece now on three needles return to the last row knitted and turn to the WS. With fourth double-pointed needle work as follows:
Needle #1 (WS): K1 (P1, K1) 3x
Needle #2 (WS): P1, place marker, K1 (P1, K1) 3x, place marker, P1
Needle #3 (WS): K the added purl-wise stitch, (P1, K1) 2x, P1, LSK2tog (this seems odd but it will allow you to stay in pattern for the ribbing that is now being worked in both directions.)

Turn to the RS. Work as follows:
Needle #3 (RS): P1, (K1, P1) 3x, place marker, YO
Needle #2 (RS): K1, YO, slip marker, P1 (K1, P1) 3x, slip marker, YO, K1
Needle #1 (RS): YO, place marker, P1, (K1, P1) 3x

Turn to WS. Continue to work in pattern for ribbing. Purl all YOs on WS. On RS continue to increase 4 stitches on each row by adding a YO on either side of the Stockinette Stitches just before or after the markers as shown in Figure 4. You will quickly see the pattern emerging. The ribbing along the edge is growing in both directions and the center back ribbing is taking shape as the body of the shawl, in Stockinette Stitch, increases in size. As your shawl grows you will want to change to a circular needle.

Continue working in this pattern until the piece measures 20" from the top of the center rib.

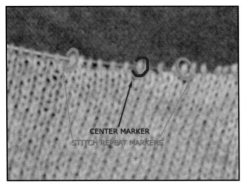

Figure 5

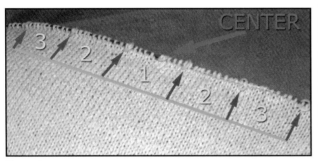

Figure 6

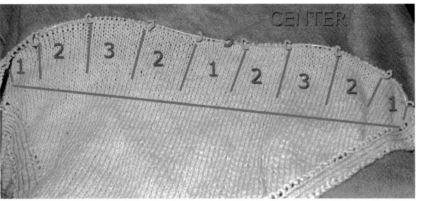

Figure 7

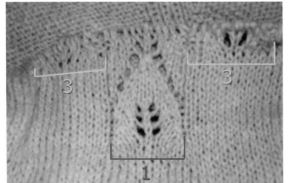

Figure 8

Planning the First Lace Pattern

Once your knitting measures 20 inches along the center back seam, it is time to begin the lace pattern. You can adjust the length more or less to suit the final dimensions that you want. I am going to explain how to plan for the Lace Patterns and then you can determine how many repeats you want on your shawl in order to get your final size. One of the reasons I resist writing out row by row instructions is because it is more difficult to make adjustments. I'd rather explain how to plan for the pattern rows and let each knitter decide for her/himself.

First: Place the Stitch Markers: On each of the two sides of the shawl, count the number of stitches on your needle and mark the center stitch (Fig. 5 in purple). Place a marker there. Then count outwards and place two more markers so that there are 11 stitches between the two markers (indicated in orange in Fig. 5). The center marker will be removed once you start working in pattern. The first lace pattern, Fin Lace, is worked over 11 stitches. Once you have marked the 11 stitches at the center continue to count outwards placing a marker after every group of 11 stitches. Do the same thing for the other side of the shawl.

Second: Count Your Sets: Once you have all the stitch markers in place you can count how many sets of 11 stitches you have to determine how you want to begin the first lace pattern. In the original Mermaid Shawl I marked the stitch sets 2121212 but in this one, because there are more stitches at this point than on the original, I am marking them 3212321232123 (Figure 7). This allows you to work the Lace Pattern gradually over three repeats of the pattern. In the 2121212 you would work a stitch set in Stockinette Stitch (2) then a set in Lace (1), then a set in Stockinette (2), etc. working so that the Lace motif was centered in the middle of each side of the shawl. If you do that the Lace Pattern is worked in over only two repeats of the pattern.

Third: Begin Working First Lace Pattern: As you resume knitting remember to continue to M1 stitch before and after the ribbing stitches on RS rows. Every time you have increased to the point that there are 11 stitches, mark that with another marker. Knit plain Stockinette in the stitch sets marked 2 and 3 but work the first Lace Pattern in the stitch sets marked 1. When a full Lace Pattern (14 rows) is complete, start the second pattern repeat working plain stockinette in stitch sets 3 only and the Lace Pattern in stitch sets 1 and 2. By the third pattern repeat, all stitch sets will be worked in Lace.

The First Lace Pattern (Fin Lace Pattern): Use the chart below to work your first Lace Pattern. Work in pattern on the RS. On WS purl in K and YO stitches, K in purl stitches.

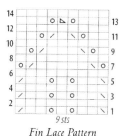

Fin Lace Pattern

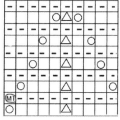

Wave Lace Pattern

A Word About / and \ ...

In the charts in this book you will see two symbols, / and \. In knitting charts they mean **K2-together-slanting-to-the-right** or **K2- together-slanting-to-the-left**. In written directions they are usually written as K2tog and SSK. Because I knit continental style that confused me for years. In written directions in this book I've adopted the habit of using **RSK2tog** and **LSK2tog**. I think that makes more sense and is easier to understand for different types of knitters. See Knitterly Notes on page 47 for more information.

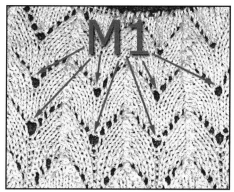

Figure 10

Figure 11

Figure 9

The Second Lace Pattern

By now you should have a pretty good idea of how this shawl works. Once you have finished 2 or 3 pattern repeats of the Fin Lace Pattern, it is time to start the second Lace Pattern—I call it the Wave Lace.

As you can see in Figure 9, there are four repeats of the Fin Lace and then the Wave Lace begins. Work as many repeats of the Wave Lace as you have decided you need, *except for the last one*. That one is worked differently. Directions follow.

Since the Wave Lace is worked over 11 stitches it should blend beautifully with the previous Lace. This is part of the beauty of this design—the way the Lace Patterns flow together. You will notice in the Wave Lace Chart at left and in Figure 10 that there is a M1 in the second (WS) row. This is to compensate for the K3tog in the first row. In order to M1 in that position K1 and then P1 in the same stitch.

When I made the first Mermaid Shawl I was working in a very fuzzy Suri alpaca that hid all of my mistakes but working with a smooth yarn which gives excellent stitch definition requires more attention to detail and precision.

If you are worried about how to work the Lace Patterns in at the four increase points (before and after the rib stitches at either side and the middle back) just keep knitting Stockinette until you have enough stitches to begin another pattern repeat. I often begin a half-repeat when I have increased enough, but this is something you will learn to do as you work. Either way is fine. Figures 9 and 11 show how I am adjusting the Lace as the shawl grows wider.

When you have achieved the depth you want *except for one pattern repeat* and the "tails" it is time to move to the final Lace Pattern.

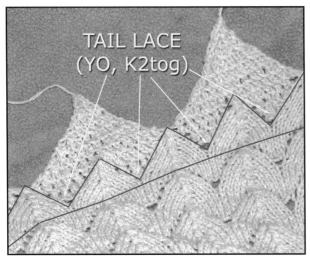

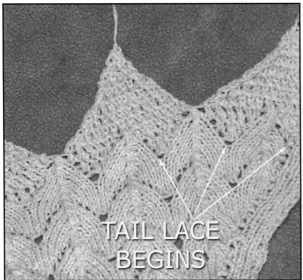

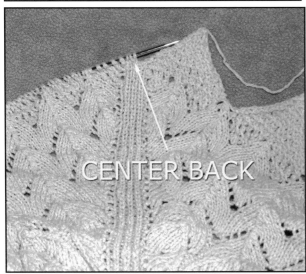

Top to bottom: Figures 12, 13, 14

Knitting the Tails

The Lace Pattern that forms the Tails is a very simple Lace: *YO, LSK2tog* on both RS and WS. That's all there is to it. In Barbara Walker's book she calls this Mermaid Lace. Where the cleverness comes in is by introducing the Tails Lace while you are also knitting the last repeat of the Waves Lace. In Figure 12, at left, you can see how this is done. As you work the Waves Lace instead of beginning another repeat between the "waves" you begin "tails" by knitting YO, LSK2tog. This will require a little bit of fudging—sometimes only knitting one stitch instead of K2 tog—but you don't have to worry about this throwing your count off because you will be binding off as each tail is completed.

On the first Mermaid Shawl, the green one, I made a Tail between each repeat of the Wave pattern but when I did that with the second shawl, because the Lace is much finer, the tails were too small so I changed it to work a Tail over every *two* Waves as you can see in the photos at left. You will have to decide which you prefer based on the weight of yarn you are using for your shawl.

When you have completed that final row of the Waves pattern it is time to work the last part of the Tails binding off as you work. On the first Tail, work back and forth in LSK2tog, YO, LSK2tog, front and back. As you can see, this decreases the number of stitches you are working with on each row until you have 2 left on your needle. Cut the thread. Loop it through and start again on the next set of stitches. You may choose to weave in the cut yarn. I decided to finish the edge with a single row of single crochet working up one side of each tail and down the other, enclosing the cut end as I worked.

As you can see in the pictures, I worked the ribbing on the 2 sides and down the back just as I would extra sets of Lace stitches. I just figured how many stitches more or less this added to each tail pattern and compensated for them. This involved knitting a couple of K stitches instead of LSK2tog on the first row to make the tails the same size. I hope this makes some kind of sense.

It is my hope that in working on your Mermaid Shawl you will gain confidence in your ability to make adjustments and decisions as you work and that you will use the decisions that you make to try another shawl using different Laces. Two examples of this follow in the Gypsy Shawl, a very simple to work shawl that shows off a distinctive yarn, and the Shawl of Falling Leaves and Shooting Stars that is best knit in a plain yarn to show off your knitting. 80Q

Both Mermaid Shawls: On the right is the original Mermaid Shawl knit from Suri alpaca on #10 needles.
On the left is the second Mermaid Shawl knit from a viscose/angora blend on #9 needles.

The Gypsy Shawl

In this closeup you can see the simplicity of this pattern. It is knit entirely of recycled sari silk. The pattern is exactly the same as the Mermaid Shawl for the first 20 inches. Then the Lace Pattern begins. This Lace, called Old Shale, is my favorite for use with yarns that have a lot of texture. It is a very simple Lace to work fol-lowing the chart below or the instructions included here. Work the Lace for the desired number of repeats until the shawl achieves the desired length. As in the Mermaid Shawl you continue to work increases on either side of the ribbing, adding pattern repeats as you work.

Directions for Old Shale Lace

Row 1 (RS): K across
Row 2 (WS): P across
Row 3 (RS): (K1, YO)3x, (LSK2tog)3x, (RSK2tog)3x, (YO, K1)2x, YO, repeat to Edge.
Row 4 (WS): K across

When you are finished you can work 2 or 3 rows of Garter Stitch and bind off or crochet a single row of single cro-chet to bind off. This makes the edge more elastic, which Lace Patterns require. 🙞🙜

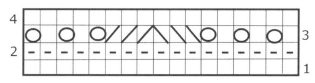

Old Shale Lace Pattern

A Shawl of Falling Leaves & Shooting Stars

This lovely shawl is knit in wool on #7 needles. It uses the same beginning as the Mermaid Shawl and consists of two Lace Patterns—Falling Leaves and Shooting Stars—and is finished with a crocheted Lace Edge. The difference in this shawl is that the first Lace Pattern, Falling Leaves, begins at the top of the shawl and is knit for 20 inches. There is a transition section of Trellis Lace and then Shooting Stars Lace begins. Shooting Stars is the name given this Lace Pattern in an old knitting book in my collection but it is virtually the same as the Lace Pattern called Frost Flowers. It appears to be very complicated when you look at the chart but it really isn't. There are actually only four pattern rows to learn—you then repeat them four times.

Begin at the center back as shown on page 9. Unlike the Mermaid and Gypsy Shawls, this one begins with Lace as soon as there are seven stitches between the markers. Follow the chart at right and work 20 inches of Falling Leaf, increasing as you work and adding new motifs as the stitches increase. In Figure 15 at right you can see the way the pattern stitches are added along the center back as the YO continue to make the shawl wider.

When the shawl is 20 inches deep (or the depth you have decided works best for you), begin Trellis Lace. This is a transitional Lace that leads into the Shooting Star Lace Pattern after 2 or 3 inches.

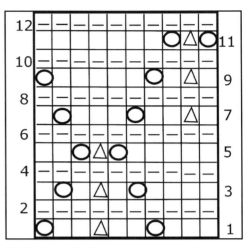

Falling Leaves Lace Pattern - Repeat 10 stitches & 12 rows

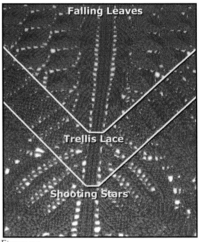

Figure 15

At the point where you want to begin the Shooting Star Lace (left), use the technique described in the Mermaid Shawl instructions to count outward from your center of each panel. Placing markers at the center of each "star" motif (the point where the LSK2tog and RSK2tog come together) worked best for me. Since the pattern shifts by 17 in the second half of the pattern, you can either mark every 17 stitches or every 34, counting from the center of the motifs.

Because the Shooting Stars pattern is wider than many Lace Patterns (34 stitches) it takes a lot more stitches to start a new pattern as the shawl widens but, as you can see in Figure 16, the stitches will form a new pattern even with a small number of decreases and YOs worked in pattern.

For the shawl pictured here I worked five pattern repeats of the Shooting Stars pattern which gave me a

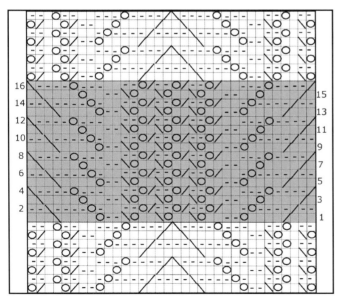

This is the graph for the beautiful Lace Pattern called Shooting Star. It looks complicated but there are actually only four rows of stitches to learn. You just repeat them four times. If you have learned the Trellis Lace Border on page 30 you already know half of them. Despite looking complicated it is four pattern rows repeated four times (pink area). Then the same four rows are shifted half a pattern repeat and again repeated four times.

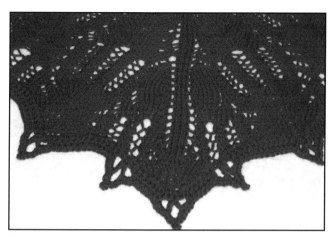

Figure 16 - Center Back

length of 40". On the last repeat of the Shooting Star Lace, work rows 1 thru 8 as indicated on the chart. As you begin row 9, bind off the 12 stitches of the Trellis Lace and work each of the last 8 rows of the "star motifs" separately. Because you continue to decrease but not make YOs, the motif will grow smaller (see chart at right). Bind off last 4 stitches, cut yarn, and begin next repeat, binding off 12, then working as above. As you can see in Figure 16, there was not a complete motif at the Center Back. However I counted 9 stitches outward from both sides of the Center Back Stitch and worked a half motif in the same manner as though finishing a motif.

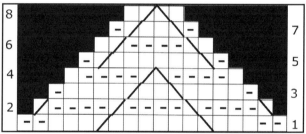

Shooting Star Border Finish - the black blocks indicate empty space.

The last three rows of this Lace are worked in crochet as follows:

Row 1 (RS): SC in all stitches. Ch 1, turn.

Row 2 (WS): SC to 2 stitches before the stitch that is at the center of the Trellis Lace motif or at the center of the Shooting Star motif, sk 2 sc. The "Point" is worked as follows: [chain 2, DBLst in center stitch of motif, skip next stitch, chain 5, DBLst in center stitch again, chain 2, skip next stitch], SC in each stitch to 2 stitches before the next motif center.

Row 3 (RS): SC in all SCs, [Work 3 SCs in chain of 2, in chain of five work 3 SCs, chain 3 then SC back into same stitch for picot, 3 SC. Work 3 SCs in end chain of 2], continue SC to next Point.

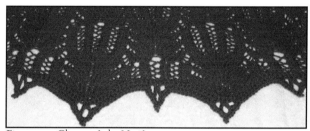

Figure 17 - Closeup of edge Motifs

A Point is worked at the very beginning and at the very end of the bottom edge (see Figure 18). For the Center Back half motif I added a Point at the beginning and end of the motif as well as one in the center. This is strictly a judgment call on my part. Each designer has to make his or her own decision. **ଛଠଔ**

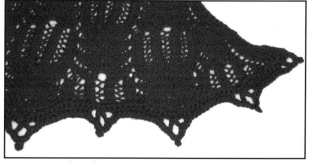

Figure 18 - Right End

THE MERMAID SHAWL:
A STORY

by Kathleen Valentine

Nights like this remind me that this island is the only place I can ever live. The nights are cold now that November is approaching but still the days stay warm. But tonight, tonight with its icy scintillation of stars and the barest hint of a moon, a thin sliver, like the charm dangling from the bracelet of one of the rich tourist ladies who come here in the summer, rides high up in the dark. The show is just beginning — a faint streak of green, a panel of rose that appears and just as swiftly shimmers away. Then pearl. Then violet. They are flirts, these lights.

When I was a little girl my father would come into my room and wake me, wrap me in blankets, and carry me half asleep and cranky on his shoulder out into the cold night.

"Look, sweetie," he would say, "it's the Aurora. You'll remember this all your life."

We lived on the south shore of the Lake then not far from a city and the night sky was not the dense black that it is here. I wonder what my father would think of the Aurora here where the night is as black as the place he now rests in. My father, professor of botany and amateur herbalist, loved the beauties of the earth and of the skies. But thinking about that will make me sad. Tonight is not a night for sadness.

"Look, sweetie," I say to my little son nestled tender and warm as a poached egg here inside my shawl, "It's the Aurora. You can watch this through the winter nights."

He burrows into me and puts his thumb in his mouth as he rubs the alpaca of my shawl against his nose. He is seconds from sleep. My little snuggly bunny. My little drowsy bug. He has watched the Aurora with me before. He has lived on this island all the three years of his young life. He does not know there is a world beyond it. I wonder how long I will be able to let him live with such a gift. How long until he knows about the world of traffic jams and constant noise, rage and rudeness, violence and fear. For now his world is pure and free of these things.

We are lucky, those of us who live out here. In the summer when the tourists arrive we get a taste of that other world. The ferries come across the Lake from Chicago or Milwaukee bearing cars and noise and chatter and rudeness. They come, the invaders, in shorts and sneakers, wearing fanny-packs filled with credit cards. We appreciate that. They crowd our shops and fill their bags as they fill our cash registers.

My shop is called The Mermaid's Shawl. Everybody wants one, a shawl knit by women on this little island far off in the icy blueness of a Great Lake where the Northern Lights fill the winter skies and sudden gales fill the bottom with hulls of ships and bones of men. There is a documentary that is shown in our local cinema each summer, The Winds of November, about those ships. The tourists all know the name Edmund Fitzgerald but that was only one of many. But I will not think of that either on a night as beautiful as this.

I came here after my father died. I had a little money and no one to worry about or to worry for me. I came to attend a knitting retreat I read about on an internet discussion board. Through the years of caring for my dying father I escaped from the day's worries by logging on to spend my nights among knitters from around the world. It was solace and distraction. It kept me sane. Every time I read about knitting retreats I dreamed of someday... And then my father died. I sold the house we had lived in all my life, counted up my assets, and left. I took only my knitting needles and my father's books. I did not know then that it would be forever.

Alma lived on this island. She had a yarn shop and taught knitting. Alma. Soul. Alma was beautiful and quiet and had magic in her hands. She touched wool or silk or alpaca or angora and suddenly it was something else. Intricate patterns as fine as spider webs, as symmetrical as the designs in a kaleidoscope. When the camp was over I couldn't bear to leave. I rented a little house and spent my days in Alma's shop watching her fingers as they danced along sticks of bamboo or rosewood. Her fingers flicked yarn over a needle and swiftly transferred stitches back and forth making patterns with pretty names — rose trellis, birch leaves, frost flowers.

Finally, she hired me to work in the shop and taught me the mystery of knitting lace that she had carried with her from another island in the Northern Seas. She told me about her island where at night you could hear the call of bagpipes from the hills of Scotland to the south. And by day you could see gold in the beards of the men fathered by the Vikings from Norway to the east.

As we sat over our needles in the dark winter nights Alma told me about festivals where a sheep would be sheared, the wool washed and spun, and knit by teams of island women, to see who could create the finest shawl before the sun went down. I brewed her pots of herbal teas gathered from the island's meadows. She talked about the shawls the women knit — so fine they could be drawn through a wedding band. She taught me about the fibers — cashmere is warmest but the price is dear. Wool is king, alpaca queen. And she told me the lore of the patterns and how women sat by firelight waiting for their men to come back from the sea as they created shawls, sweaters, and counterpanes in patterns called shooting star, falling leaf, lily of the valley, traveling vine.

Sometimes a man did not come back. Then his woman knit her sorrow into a mourning shawl and wore it to remember him.

"A woman who loses a man to the sea never really stops waiting," Alma said. "Every time a cry goes round the village, that the shape of a man has been spotted on the shore, her heart leaps. She prays. She thinks, 'maybe I will be the lucky one'." Alma sighed.

She took me to the saddest place on this island then. It is in the corner of our only cemetery. Tucked away in one corner under scrub pine are thirty-three headstones, plain and unremarkable with sad inscriptions — "Seaman, about 25, April 12, 1889". Some have names but mostly each just reads "seaman" and a date. These are the bodies of the mariners washed ashore since the island was first inhabited. Unless something in their clothing told their name, no one knew. The islanders brought them here for burial.

Alma said a prayer for their souls. I said a prayer for the women who were in another place waiting, the women who never knew.

"I think it is a blessing that you came here," Alma said during my third summer on the island. She had hired local women to spin for her and we dyed yarns with dyes made from the island's plentiful vegetation. They were growing in popularity. I purchased a computer for the shop and began a web site to sell her yarns and patterns on the internet during the quiet, frozen winter months. An internet business would improve our chances of surviving each winter. But then she said the words I was not prepared to hear.

"I think it might be time for me to go back home."

No, I told her, you can't leave the island. But I knew when the summer season ended she would leave us. And I knew that I would buy her shop.

She left in September with the last of the tourist ferries. I walked with her to the dock and hugged her, promising to take good care of her shop and her yarns and to share the patterns with all who wanted to learn them. The winter would be bleak without her. Or would have been had it not been for the stranger.

October brought winds and ice-filled muzzlers howling down from the North Pole and swooping across Lake Superior slapping at barges and upending fishing tugs. It was old Chinook Luther who spotted him tangled up in the mess on the rocks. Lucky for the stranger Chinook Luther's wife Lucille hadn't seen him sneaking out to go fishing that morning. She would have told him "t'is not a fit day out for man nor beast" and hidden his boots in the pantry behind the jars of applesauce that she had just put up. But Chinook wanted one more walleye before the cove iced in and it was Chinook's longing for bass that saved the stranger's life.

I was on the headlands that morning walking back from having coffee with one of my spinners. I had a basket full of fine, lace-weight wool ready for the dye-pot when I saw Chinook bicycling furiously toward me.

"Man on the rocks," he bellowed his great walrus moustache dripping sea-spray, "man on the rocks. I'm gone for help."

I ran, slipping in the wet marsh grasses and slid down the dunes. There was an outcrop of rock that jutted out into the Lake, like a protective finger, curved around the cove. I dropped my basket and scrambled across the rocks, frigid water splashing into my boots and soaking my jeans. The rocks were slick with seaweed and moss and I was glad I'd put on leather gloves but by the time I reached him they were soaked as well. I lay across the rocks and grabbed the back of his jacket pulling him farther up onto the rocks out of the icy sea. Chinook had flown on his bike. Men were already running down the beach. The stranger was nearly frozen but, as I tugged again, pulling him higher, he moaned.

"He's alive," I screamed and the wind carried my voice to the men running toward us. "He's alive."

What wonderful words, I thought later. He's alive.

I tore off my gloves and pressed my hand to his throat feeling for a pulse, trying to sense its strength. My hands were cold but not as cold as he was and his eyelids twitched. He looked at me and I was startled by the warmth of gold-flecked brown eyes.

"It's okay," I said, pressing my hand to his cheek. "Help is coming. You'll be all right."

His eyes stayed locked onto mine as though I was a life raft. His lips moved and I leaned down to hear his words.

"Mermaid," he whispered.

They carried him to the rectory of the island chapel. We don't have a hospital anymore. There are a few EMTs and the Reverend Gorske's wife worked as a nurse practitioner before they moved out here in semi-retirement. The weather would not permit a helicopter to the mainland and another storm was on the way so we cared for him as most sick or injured on this island are cared for, patiently, lovingly and with as much expertise as we can pull together. Those of us who believe in prayer used that, too. And, as is the case often enough to make it seemed justified, those things appeared to be what was needed.

We took turns sitting with him. I made warm infusions of mullein, marsh mallow, linden flower, and horsetail to bathe his chest and throat and face. He was a beautiful young man — dark and long of limb with black hair and copper skin. His body was scarred and Lucille Luther said he must have been at sea all his life. She recognized the patterns of assaults on tender flesh, the hazards of a seaman's life. He slept and he slept and he slept.

In the late afternoon as the light was beginning to fade, I came to sit with him. When he was able to sip a little, I made him elderflower and mullein tea. He was so weak it pained me. Still, his heart seemed strong. He spoke barely at all but when his eyes opened and rested on me he always whispered the same thing, "My mermaid."

That was how I began the first shawl. I retrieved the basket of wool from the headlands where I dropped it that day and chose to dye it in a bath of mullein, too, using copper sulfate as a mordant and mixing in lichen gathered from the rocks along the beach to create a soft aquamarine wool. I studied Alma's books of lace patterns and selected the ones I wanted — fish scales, fins, and a fine mesh known as mermaid's tail.

In the darkening afternoon, as I sat beside his bed I worked on my shawl. I knit into it the fragrance of the fields on the headlands and the lichen on the shore. I knit into it the strength of male arms lifting one of their fellow mariners from the clutches of the sea. I knit into it the warmth of women's hands as they bathed him and cared for him and lifted his beautiful dark head to spoon soup and tea between his cracked and bleeding lips. I knit into it our hopes and our prayers for him, our fear that we would lose him — this stranger whose name we did not know. I knit into it blessings for all the men who lived their lives at sea, especially the ones snatched from their ships by the Lake, especially the ones in the quiet sad corner of our cemetery, those mariners who never went home again. I sat beside his bed, watching him breathe, knitting my shawl remembering what Alma taught me — every stitch is a prayer.

By the time the solstice came we knew we had succeeded in saving this one mariner from a nameless sailor's grave. He stayed awake for longer periods. He watched us and smiled. He began to speak a little and it was then that we discovered he knew very little English. His name was Sergei, he said. He worked a cargo ship out of Poland. He knew he had been swept overboard in a storm. He did not know what happened to his ship. He was shy, grateful, polite, sweet. He kept his eyes on me.

"Don't you go falling in love," Lucille frowned at me. "I seen the way he looks at you. Don't you go believing it."

But it was too late.

Chinook Luther took me aside. "If the Lake had him once, she'll have him ag'in. You can't take a man from a jealous lady like that there Lake is."

But I thought that was pure romanticism.

"We need to get this boy back where he belongs," the Reverend Gorske told me. "I'm calling the Coast Guard."

But I didn't listen. When he was strong enough to walk I took him home with me and we spent the long winter nights watching the Aurora sweeping across the big, dark sky and keeping each other warm. He was mine, I thought, I gathered him from the sea like I gathered herbs and flowers from the meadows. He was mine.

And all during those nights when he held me and touched me and whispered his sweet, strange words in my ear, I recognized only two. "My mermaid," he said, "my mermaid."

My shawl was just finished when the Coast Guard men came. With them was an INS officer. He had to return to the mainland and be sent home. His family would be so glad to know he was alive. He could return to work on another ship. He could come back but they had to follow procedure. Those were the rules.

I went with him to the Coast Guard cutter. I wore the mermaid shawl and he wrapped it tight around me as he kissed me goodbye.

"I come back," he said. "You wait, my mermaid, I come back."

"I know you will," I said.

I waited until the ship disappeared from sight, then I walked back to my shop. Spring was coming and the meadows would be filled with herbs. In the remaining weeks of winter dark I busied myself with the web site. Orders for hand-dyed yarns were coming in. I had been too besotted to pay attention. It was good to have the work to do, but every night I lay in bed alone, watching the Aurora which would be leaving soon too. I wrapped the shawl around me and pretended it was him.

Out of loneliness I wrote the story of my shawl and why I made it. I told about the beautiful stranger I pulled from the sea and nursed with herbs and prayers. I posted the story on my web site. Soon emails arrived asking for pictures. I draped my mermaid shawl across the rocks where I had pulled my beloved from the sea, photographed it, and posted those too. More email came. Would I sell the pattern? Would I sell the shawl? Everyone loved my story. Everyone wanted a mermaid shawl like mine. I needed something to devote myself to while I waited and so I changed the name of Alma's shop for him. I wrote down the instructions for him. I hired more women to knit shawls to sell — for him.

This is what I came to believe: when you do something from love it makes magic. That love flows out of you into everything you do and infuses the fruit of your hands like the herbs from the meadow infuse the wool with their colors. People, ever-yearning, are drawn by all that love. They long to take part in it in any way they can.

My little son yawns and whispers, "Cold, mommy." I have promised he will never have to be cold. I carry him into the house and tuck him into bed, cuddle his soft, hand-knit blankets around him and brush his black hair away from his sweet, small face. His eyes flicker open, struggling against sleep. They are warm brown eyes with flecks of gold. When I look into them I hear the echo of long-ago words, "My mermaid". I kiss him and tuck his blankets around him but his eyes have already drifted shut in sleep.

I turn out the lights and pick up my knitting and go to sit by the window and wait. He will come back. He told me so. I begin work on another mermaid shawl and watch the pattern of lace spill from my needles. He will come back.

ಸಿ)(ೞ

Emily's Shawl knit of fingering-weight merino wool and angora on #6 needles. Shown at left with a shawl pin made by Leslie Wind and below worn by the shawl's inspiration, my niece Emily

Photo by: Paula Ryan

EMILY'S SHAWL:
ENDLESS VERSATILITY

I made this shawl for my niece Emily. It is knit of a fine, fingering weight blend of wool and angora that I bought at a spinners gathering in Camden, Maine some years ago. The design is a classic design that has appeared in many magazines and books. Once you learn the technique you can make it over and over using different lace patterns to create different looks. It is consistently lovely and can be made out of delicate fibers or sock yarn.

The technique used for these shawls is not only a classic but has several advantages. It can be as plain or as fancy as you want it to be, you can experiment with several Lace Patterns, and once the center panel is knit, you then knit-in-the-round so your pattern is always facing you. It is excellent with Lace Patterns that have pattern stitches on both the RS and the WS as well as patterns that alternate with plain knit rounds.

The truth is the first time I used this technique, with Beth's Shawl, it was a bit of an accident. Most of my best creations happen that way. I had four good-sized balls of lovely, fine 50% cashmere/50% silk from China in two shades of blue and two shades of violet. I decided to work two strands together and, as with the Shimmer Shawl, to alternate overlapping color changes, as described on page 3, to give a softer changeover. I chose Ostrich Plume for the center panel because it is a beautiful all-over Lace Pattern and would stand up to the changes in color. When the shawl was long enough I still had a fair amount of yarn left so I decided to pick up stitches around the perimeter of the shawl, marking the four corners, and knit in the round. I chose my old reliable pattern Old Shale. The results were lovely.

Beth's Shawl

After making a few swatches and trying different size needles I decided that I liked #7 needles and that I needed 6 repeats of Ostrich Plume Lace which is 16 stitches for each repeat. The Trellis Lace Border (page 30) was my choice for the Border:

10 + 96 (16 pattern stitches x 6 repeats) + 10 = 116 stitches

Beth's Shawl knit in cashmere/silk blend on #7 Needles

Holding 2 strands together cast on 116 stitches. Work 2 K rows. Knit 10 stitches in Trellis Lace, place marker, knit 6 repeats of Ostrich Plume Lace (see chart on page 21), place marker. Knit final 10 stitches in Trellis Lace. The WS rows of Ostrich Plume Lace are all purled.

When the Main Panel is as long as you would like it to be, finish with 2 K rows and bind off.

With a #7 24"-circular needle, pick up stitches around the perimeter of the shawl. Do this by picking up

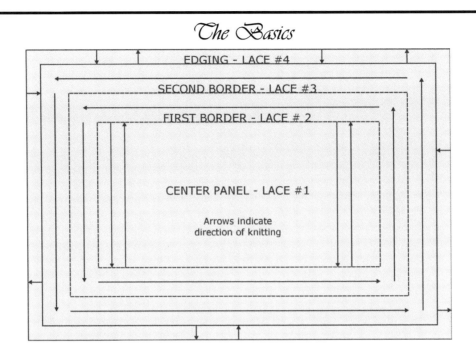

The Basics

EDGING - LACE #4

SECOND BORDER - LACE #3

FIRST BORDER - LACE # 2

CENTER PANEL - LACE #1

Arrows indicate
direction of knitting

All of the shawls in the Rectangular Shawl Section follow this diagram. You can use 2 or 3 lace patterns plus a lace Edging. The construction is fairly simple as it is all knit in one piece. The Center Panel is knit in one long rectangle. Pick up the stitches around the edge of the center panel on a circular needle, making sure to mark the four corners. Start second lace pattern and knit around and around in pattern until you are ready to change to the third lace pattern. When you decide you are finished, you then add on the Edging using straight needles and picking up stitches from the circular needle as you work.

one stitch for every stitch knit on the two ends and four stitches for every 5 rows on the length-wise sides. *Make sure to place a stitch marker at each of the four corners of the piece.* The four corners will be increased as follows:

Work in pattern to the marker. YO, slip marker, K1, YO. Repeat on all four sides. Increase on alternating rows. On the second row: work in pattern, K1 in YO, slip marker, K2.

As your piece increases in size you may begin new repeats of the pattern as you are able. If you are working the Border in Old Shale you will be working in the round, unlike the Gypsy Shawl. Thus:

Directions for Old Shale Lace in the Round:

Row 1 (RS): K around

Row 2 (WS): K around

Row 3 (RS): (K1, YO)3x, (LSK2tog)3x, (RSK2tog)3x, (YO, K1)2x, YO, repeat around.

Row 4 (WS): P around

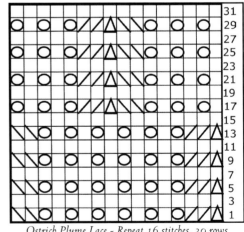

Ostrich Plume Lace - Repeat 16 stitches, 30 rows

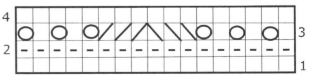

Old Shale Lace - Repeat: 17 stitches & 4 rows

The Border on Beth's Shawl consists of 24 rows in pattern and then 2 rows of plain knitting. It is finished with a single row of single crochet. ✍

A Note on Planning the Size of Your Main Panel

Deciding the overall size of your shawl in advance can help you decide how wide you want the Main Panel to be and how long. It is a matter of proportion but the math is fairly simple. Imagine your ideal shawl size is 72" long by 30" wide. And you have decided that you want a 10" Border. That means that you have to deduct 10 inches from each of the 4 sides of the shawl thus:

Width: 30" - 20" (10 inches for each side) = 10" wide

Length: 72" - 20" (10 inches for each side) = 52" long

Therefore, you will cast on the number of stitches you need (which you know from your swatch) to make your center panel 10" wide and you will continue to knit until the piece is 52" long. Then you will pick up the stitches around the perimeter and knit for 10" all around. Your finished piece will be 72" x 30".

Also please note that it is not necessary to knit a Border on the Main Panel. I did, but that was because I decided to add the Border later. It is customary to knit the Main Panel without the Border, knitting the chosen pattern from one edge to the other.

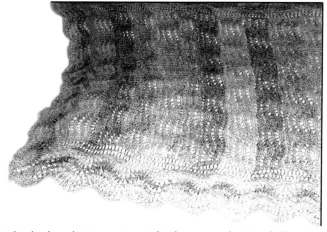

This shawl was knit for my sister Beth. The center panel is Ostrich Plume, like Emily's Shawl, and the Border is Old Shale, like the Gypsy Shawl.

Emily's Shawl

While Beth's Shawl is long and narrow, Emily's Shawl is wider so that it can be folded when worn or so it can double as a throw. My purpose in creating this shawl was to try a variety of laces and techniques. The center panel is also knit in Ostrich Plume (chart on facing page) but it would be equally lovely in a pattern such as Rose Trellis, Falling Leaves or any of the other beautiful patterns found in the many knitted Lace treasureries by

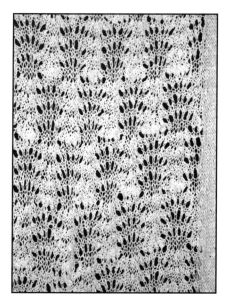

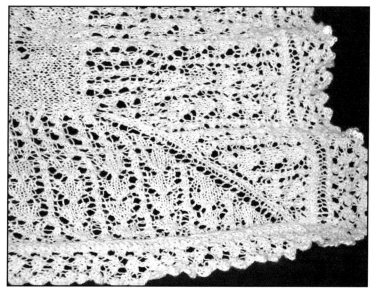

Closeups of the patterns used. The center panel is Ostrich Plume with a Garter Stitch Border. After the center panel was complete, a circular needle was used to pick up stitches around the perimeter with a marker added at each of the four corners. A delicate pattern called Little Leaf was worked for four pattern rounds then the third lace pattern, Snowdrop, was begun. As you can see the corners were mitered. When the third pattern was complete, the piece ws bound off and a knitted-on lace edge was worked all the way around the perimeter.

Barbara Walker, Marianne Kinzel, and others. In one of Marianne Kinzels' books she has a Lace Pattern she calls Lilac Time which I have been dreaming about. I have some laceweight cashmere in a color called "Lilac". I keep dreaming about a rectangular shawl using the motifs in her Lilac Time designs but laid-out according to this diagram.

My point being that you should have fun planning your shawls. Take a few books with Lace Patterns and sit down with a cup of coffee or tea and daydream. Imagine which patterns might look nice together. I find it is best to use an all-over Lace Pattern like Ostrich Plume or Rose Trellis for the center then add a pattern that repeats in stripe-like columns for the Border—Horseshoe Lace or Snowdrop are two of my favorites.

With Emily's Shawl I cast on 116 stitches, 10 for each Border and 96 for the Main Panel:

10 + 96 (16 pattern stitches x 6 repeats) + 10 = 116 stitches

I decided to work the Border in plain Garter Stitch so knit 8 rows in Garter Stitch before beginning the pattern. I worked seven repeats of the 32 row pattern (222 rows) then 8 rows of Garter Stitch to finish.

I knew that I wanted to try two Lace Patterns for the Border. For Lace #1 I chose Little Leaf. It is a small, simple, lovely pattern that makes a nice transition lace. Following the method for creating the mitered corners described on page 22, I picked up stitches around the

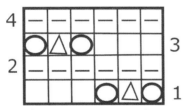

Little Leaf Lace - Repeat: 6 stitches & 4 rows

perimeter. I decided to use 2 K stitches to form the miter point (YO, K2, YO) at each of the four corners. This is an arbitrary choice and just depends on your taste. Sometimes I use 1, sometimes 3. The choice is yours. My general rule is the finer the yarn, the fewer the stitches that form the corners (miter points).

The Lace #1 pattern is worked on six stitches, *(K3, YO, K3tog, YO) repeat*. Because you are working in the round, every other row is, technically the WS row so all stitches are knit (K) with *no* yarn overs (YOs). For Emily's Shawl I worked five repeats of the pattern and

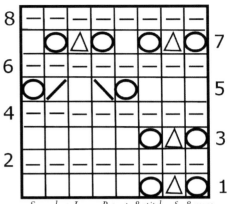

Snowdrop Lace - Repeat: 8 stitches & 8 rows

then switched to Lace #2, Snowdrop Lace (Chart above). Since this Lace is worked on a multiple of 8 stitches, the transition worked easily.

As you can see in the photgraph on page 23, additional repeats of the pattern were added as the shawl grew outward. After five repeats of Lace #2, the shawl was ready to be finished.

One of the things to be mindful of when knitting Lace is that the beauty of the Lace often depends on binding off with lots of flexibility so the bind-off does not prevent the Lace from stretching as it is blocked. This is why Lace is often finished with a crochet edge that allows for lots of stretch or is "knitted off" with a Lace Border. Some knitters change to needles 2 or 3 sizes larger than those they have used for the piece to knit the last 2 rows and the bind off. However, the prettiest finishes, in my opinion, are accomplished by using an edge Lace design and "knitting off".

The design I chose for Emily's Shawl is my own variation of Lover's Knot. See Chart below:

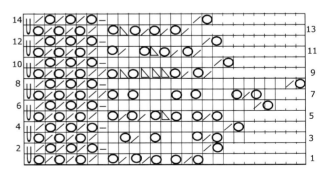

Lover's Knot Edge - This can be a challenge but I hope the directions will not confuse you. The elongated U is where the last stitch in the Edging joins the main body of Lace. The gray boxes are non-existent stitches.

This Sampler Shawl was knit to try different stitches. It was knit with one strand of mohair and one of silk held together on #10 needles.

To knit-off, keep the piece on the circular needle and place a point protector over one end of the needle. Using one straight needle in the same size and the other end of the circular needle, work back and forth on the Lace Edge. Pick up one stitch from the perimeter of the shawl and knit it together with the last (left) stitch of the Edge Lace, slipping off the stitches as you work.

Since the Edge Lace requires 14 rows to complete a repeat, and since I wanted to add a little ease at the corners, I counted the number of stitches I had around the perimeter which was 3,068. Divided by 14, that meant I had to make 220 repeats of the Edge Lace which would mean I had 12 extra rows to work. I solved this problem by working three extra rows into each of the corners, thus providing a little ease and making the row count come out even.

When the entire perimeter is worked and slipped off the needle, graft the last row of the Edge Lace to the beginning row. ✂

A Sampler Stole or Shawl

The violet mohair shawl shown in the photos on this page was one of my very first attempts at Lace knitting. It was an experiment to both try out various Lace Patterns and to test which would be adaptable to a textured yarn. As you add Lace stitch patterns to your repertoire of accomplishments you will find some stitches are best used for yarns with high stitch definition and some are beautiful no matter where they are used. With this shawl I sat down with a book of Lace Patterns and started knitting. When I felt like changing to a new pattern I knit a few rows of Garter Stitch as a break between changes. As the shawl grew I decided to reverse the order of patterns I had done in order to balance it but, I promise you, this was all done by instinct and whim with no preconceived design in mind.

Knitting Lace is an art form like any other. Once you learn the basics of your craft—whether it is how to read music, how to use and mix paint, or how to construct a sentence, the real joy of the art is in taking the discipline and craft you have acquired and then letting your imagination run wild. That is the beginning of all creativity. Please do not be so concerned with perfection that you become fearful of being creative. Perfection comes with repetition but there is no substitute for experimentation. And with yarn there are very few times when something cannot be ripped out. Starting over is good! ✂

Rose Shearwater Wrap knit of an alpaca/silk on #7 needles

Sampler Stole knit of one strand of mohair and one of silk on #10 needles

Shimmer Stole knit with double strands of alpaca/silk lace-weight on #7 needles

Silk Chenille Stole knitted with a delicate rayon/silk chenille on #2 needles

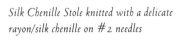

STOLES, SCARVES, WRAPS FROM ONE GREAT SHAPE

The long rectangle can be adjusted by both length and width to create anything from a pretty little scarf to accent the neckline of a jacket to a long, extravagant stole to wrap up in on chilly evenings, or to go out in on festive ones. A simple diagram and a few tricks and tips can be the basis for endless knitting variety and adventure.

With the mastery of very few stitches, this design can produce endless satisfying variations. When I see a gorgeous yarn that I can't live without but which is also pricey, a couple skeins and this design always yields a delight to work on and a pleasure to give. The diagram on the next page shows placement for three Lace Patterns but a lovely project can be created with only one, such as the Shimmer Stole, the Scrap Bag Stole, and the Silk Roving Wrap, all of which have plain Edging and Borders.

By adding the simple Trellis Lace Border described on the next page and varying the Lace designs in the Main Panel, you can make endless beauties while matering new Lace Patterns. The Blue Tulip Wrap has plain Garter Stitch Edges, Trellis Lace Borders, and a main panel in Tulip Lace. When you are ready to challenge your skills you can try the three Lace designs which include Lace Edges on both ends of the piece, Lace Border patterns and a main panel of Lace. The Silk Chenille Stole and the Rose Shearwater Wrap use this method.

If you only have a few skeins, this is ideal for a scarf like the Traveling Vine Scarf on page 36. I had four balls of a lush alpaca/cashmere so I knit a few rows of Garter Stitch for the Edge and then began the Traveling Vine Pattern with a simple 1x1 rib edge worked on four stitches. If you have an ample supply of yarn you can make something as luxurious as the Shimmer Stole which measures 32" x 72" plus fringe. It's up to you.

One of the problems knitters sometimes face when working with a limited supply of yarn is how to make the most of what they have available and still have enough yarn left to make a pretty Edge on both ends of their piece. This is something that perplexed me for awhile and resulted in lots of ripping out to start the Edge over—or a good deal of leftover yarn. Then I hit on

the idea of knitting both Edges first. Knit an Edge in the Lace Pattern of choice (I find Old Shale a lovely and useful Edge Lace). You can actually knit the Edge as deep as you like because you don't have to worry about not having enough for the end-side. In the photo below you can see the beginning of the Rose Shearwater Wrap. Three repeats of Old Shale with Trellis Lace Border was knit and then bound off and put aside. A second Border was knit and then the Shearwater Lace began. I had six balls of the yarn and no idea how far it would go but, because I had the second Edge put aside, I could knit until I ran out of yarn and not worry about it.

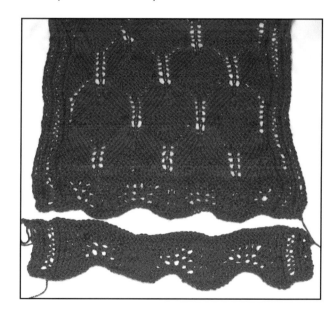

Drunk with power thanks to this new discovery, I decided to carry it a step farther. I had a substantial ball of 100% pure silk yarn from England. It is unique in that it is 2 strands of laceweight in blue and 2 in violet wound

The Basics

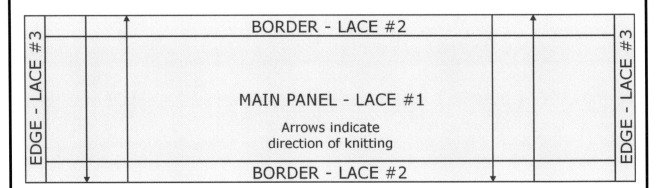

All of the shawls in the Rectangular Stole Section follow this diagram. This is the simplest construction, working back and forth for the length of the piece. There is a Main Panel in your dominant lace pattern, a Border constructed of simple lace Edging that will not roll, and an Edge lace with a clever little trick.

My Favorite Border

When selecting a Lace Pattern for the Border it is important to choose one that will not roll. This is a common problem with stockinette stitch. It is perfectly fine to create a Border with plain Garter (K all stitches) or Moss (RS: K1,P1 - WS: P in P stitches, K in K stitches) however the following lacy stitch is my favorite. It is worked over 10 stitches on either side:

Trellis Border Lace:

Right Border:
RS: (K2, YO, LSK2tog) 2x, P1, K1, place marker (to begin Main Panel Lace)
WS: Slip marker, P1, K1 (P2, YO, P2tog) 2x

Left Border:
RS: Slip marker, K1, P1, (K2, YO, LSK2tog) 2x
WS: (P2, YO, P2tog) 2x, K1, P1

This makes a neat, distinctive Border as seen in the Blue Tulip Wrap and the Rose Shearwater Wrap photos.

Reverse stitches in gray box for opposite Border.

together. The ball has been in my stash for years but I never knew what to do with it because I had no idea how far it would go. For the piece in the photo below I began by knitting a fancy Edging Lace I found online. I knit two strips 16" long and bound them off. Then I picked up

the stitches along the length of one piece and knit several rows of 18 repeats of the Trellis Edge Lace (at left) for a few inches and bound it off again. I did the same to the second length and then decided to switch to another Lace Pattern for the main panel, keeping one repeat of the Trellis Lace on either side for the Border. I don't know how long this piece will end up being but when I run out of yarn I can just bind off and sew on the second Border!
80G8

Shimmer Stole

This luxurious wrap began with the purchase of 8 skeins of laceweight alpaca/silk in four colorways. After starting a variety of projects I wanted to use all four of the colorways together in one garment. I decided to work with two strands together with alternating changes as described on page 3. So this is how I made this—you can make it as wide or as narrow as you wish. I wanted the Border, which is Garter Stitch to be 6 stitches wide on each side. The Little Leaf Pattern repeats over 6 stitches (see chart below) so I needed:

6 + 120 (6 pattern stitches x 20 repeats) + 6 = 132 stitches

Holding 2 strands together, cast on 132 stitches. Work in Garter Stitch (K all rows) for 16 rows. Begin pattern:
Row 1 (RS): K 6, place marker (to indicate Border), (K3, YO, K3tog, YO) as many times as you need to within 6 stitches of the end, place marker, K6
Row 2 (WS): K6, slip marker, P to marker, slip marker, K6
Row 3 (RS): K 6, slip marker, (YO, K3tog, YO, K3) to marker, slip marker, K6
Row 4 (WS): K6, slip marker, P to marker, slip marker, K6

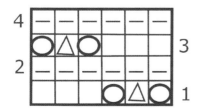

Little Leaf Lace - Repeat: 6 stitches & 4 rows

As you work you will change colors by breaking one of the two strands at whatever intervals you choose. Continue in this manner until the desired length is achieved. Work 18 rows of Garter Stitch for the end Edge, bind off. You may add fringe if you like. ⛟

Scrap Bag Stole

Every knitter accumulates odds and ends of yarn and, if you are like most knitters, you hang on to them forever. What I find helpful is to sort them according to color and store them in zip-top bags. When I am looking for an easy, fun project, I sort through my odds and ends and pull out a selection of yarns that look good together and will work in terms of weight or texture. In the Scrap Bag Stole above, I used eight balls of leftover yarn in a variety of fibers—silk, cotton, wool, and alpaca—and textures.

The pattern is all Old Shale with a simple 5-stitch rib for the Border (K1, P1, K1, P1, K1). After experimenting, I decided on #8 needles. After measuring and figuring how wide I wanted the stole to be I knew I wanted five repeats of the Old Shale Pattern which is 17 stitches wide. With 5 stitches for each Border that meant I needed:

5+17+17+17+17+17+5=95 stitches

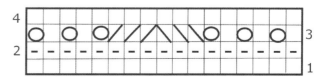

Old Shale Lace - Repeat: 17 stitches & 4 rows

Cast on 95 stitches. Work 6 rows in Garter Stitch (K all rows) for the Edge. Begin Main Panel with a 5-stitch rib on either side. Working with the Old Shale pattern as follows:

Row 1 (RS): K across

Row 2 (WS): P across

Row 3 (RS): (K1, YO)3x, (LSK2tog)3x, (RSK2tog)3x, (YO, K1)2x, YO, repeat to Edge.

Row 4 (WS): K across

Change colors, weaving in the ends as you work. You can make the stripes all the same width or change as you please. You can also work with 2 or 3 yarns held together if you would like to combine lace-weight and finger-weight yarns with thicker yarns. When the stole has achieved a length that you like, or you run out of yarn, K 6 rows of Garter Stitch and bind off.

That's all there is to it. Old Shale is an excellent stitch for a project that involves a variety of yarns because it does not require much in the way of stitch definition to show up nicely. ❧

Silk Roving Wrap

The same basic design was used for the Silk Roving Wrap, the only difference being that the edges on both ends were knit deeper with approximately 12 rows of Garter Stitch and the 2 Borders were also Garter

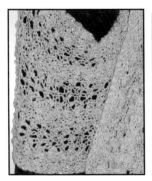 

Stitch instead of Rib and are 12 stitches wide. The Main Panel is also Old Shale.

This is a unique garment because it is knit from 100% silk unraveled from an oversized designer sweater purchased in a thrift shop. As discussed on page 3, it came as quite a surprise when I began unraveling it and discovered that the fiber had not been spun but was more like roving. It was strong and lusterous but rather shaggy

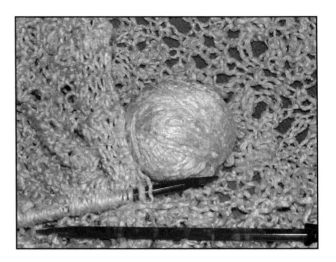

(see photo on page 3). As I unraveled the sweater, taking care to cut out the worn places, I realized however I used it, it would have to be knit loosely. I tried plain Garter Stitch but wanted something a bit lacier. The original sweater had been knit entirely in stockinette. I tried my most reliable pattern for textured yarn, Old Shale, and loved the way it looked.

One of the joys of making a garment like this is that it is both creative and highly unusual. And it has the added benefit of reusing fiber that might otherwise be thrown away. There are a number of online vendors who scour thrift stores for high quality knit garments, clean the garments, unravel them, and sell the yarn. I purchased several lots of pure silk from one of these vendors, all in soft, natural shades—ivory, taupe, pale rose, etc.—and began crocheting them into Granny Squares which I plan to sew into a jacket. But that's another book.

There is a lot of joy in reclaiming fiber of very high quality. It lets knitters work with fibers they might not otherwise be able to afford. It supplies an income for the people who recycle the fiber. It creates beautifully unique garments, and it is environmentally friendly. With a little creativity many of these recycled fibers can be transformed into one-of-a-kind masterpieces.

Try knitting the Scrap Bag Stole in compatible shades of recycled cashmere or silk for a genuine treasure. ❧

Silk Chenille Stole

The yarn for this shawl was discovered on a shelf in the warehouse at Webs in Northampton, Massachusetts. It is a fine chenille in a blend of silk and rayon in a lovely color called "Pearl". I brought it home and experimented with it for several months. One of the first things you learn when you knit with chenille is that it loves to "worm". The center fiber that holds the chenille together can twist out of shape and wiggle its way out of the newly knitted fabric creating annoying little "worms". Cotton chenille, I am told, does not do this, but rayon worms easily. There are two possible solutions—either knit the yarn with a second "carrier" yarn that has some texture to it, such as mohair, or knit tight on small needles. For that reason I selected #2 needles. There are four Lace Patterns used in this stole: Hummingbird Lace for the 2 Edges, Trellis Lace for the Borders, and Horseshoe Lace for the Main Panel with each repeat being separated by a delicate little Insertion Lace.

Cast on 92 stitches. K 3 rows, P 4th (WS) row.

Begin Hummingbird Lace (chart below left). This is a simple Lace that is easy to learn and gives a pretty effect. It is called Hummingbird because of the way it flits back and forth.

Row 1 (RS): K1, (K1, YO, K2, LSK2tog, RSK2tog, K2, YO) 10x, K1
Row 2 (WS): P
Row 3 (RS): K1, (YO, K2, LSK2tog, RSK2tog, K2, YO, K1) 10x, K1
Row 4 (WS): P
Repeat 6 times.
This Lace creates a scalloped edge that is quite nice.

When you have completed 6 repeats of the pattern (feel free to make more if you like) K one row and place stitch markers: K9, marker, {K9, marker, K4, marker} 5x, K 9, marker, K8, turn and purl back then begin your pattern. (Please note: If you are going to knit both Edges and save one as described at the beginning of the chapter bind off at this point, set Lace aside, and begin the second Edge.)

The Insertion Lace is a simple little pattern:
RS: K2, YO, K2tog
WS: P2, YO, P2tog

The Horseshoe Lace is quite easy as well. For all RS rows follow the chart below and for all WS rows purl across.

Work the pattern as follows:
{Insertion Lace} 2x, {RS P1/WS K1}, {Horseshoe Lace, Insertion Lace} 5x, Horseshoe Lace, {RS P1/WS K1}, {Insertion Lace} 2x
Work in this manner until the pattern reaches the desired length then work a plain K row (RS), P row (WS) and begin the final edge or bind off and attach the Edge that

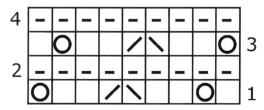

Hummingbird Lace - Repeat: 9 stitches & 4 rows

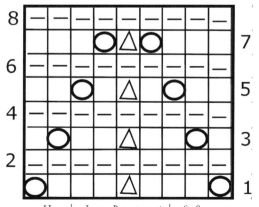

Horseshoe Lace - Repeat: 9 stitches & 8 rows

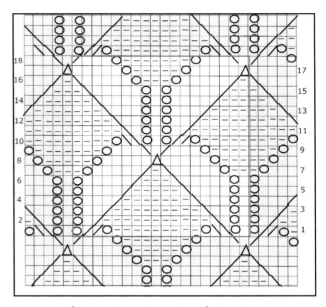

Shearwater Lace - Repeat: 18 stitches & 18 rows

Rose Shearwater Wrap

My friend Leslie said the Lace Pattern in this wrap reminded her of shearwaters swooping over the water so we are calling this Shearwater Lace. It is made from 6-110 yd. skeins of DK-weight alpaca/silk yarn on #7 needles and was knit using the technique described on page 27 of knitting both Edges first. The Borders are both Trellis Lace as described at the beginning of the chapter. After swatching I figured three repeats of the Shearwater Lace would be perfect. Because that is 18 stitches wide it meant I needed to begin with 74 stitches:

Since I intended to knit the Edges in Old Shale this presented a little challenge because Old Shale is worked on 17 stitches. This meant I had an extra three stitches to make up for. I solved the problem by adding one stitch to each pattern repeat of Old Shale as follows:

Row 1 (RS): K across
Row 2 (WS): P across
Row 3 (RS): (K1, YO)3x, (LSK2tog)3x, K1, (RSK2tog)3x, (YO, K1)2x, YO
Row 4 (WS): K across

This is a slight cheat but is the sort of solution where a little bit of creativity and innovation helps.

Cast on 74 stitches and knit four rows in Garter Stitch. On last row place markers:

K10, marker, (K18, marker) 3x

Begin the Edge with Trellis Border on either side and 3 repeats of Old Shale. For my wrap I knit 3 repeats both vertically and horizontally but, as always, I encourage you to use your own creativity! Knit 4 more rows of Garter Stitch and bind off loosely for the opposite end Edge or begin the Shearwater Pattern.

Using Markers is always tricky. Many Lace Patterns have clearly defined places where a marker can go. But there are patterns like the Shearwater Lace in which the placement of markers becomes problematic when you need to knit or purl 2 stitches together. My solution, when I can't find 2 stitches in a pattern that do not overlap, is to just move the markers as I work. I'd rather do some shifting back and forth than work without markers and run the risk of completely losing track of where I am. It is sad but true that, as I am growing older, I don't remember things like I used to. My theory about this is that I've gotten to the point where there is just so much stuff in my head new stuff gets lost in the jumble. But I digress.

The chart above for Shearwater Lace shows how the overall pattern is worked. The shaded areas are repeats of the stitches shown in white so you can get an idea of how the pattern flows together. Once you have established 2 vertical repeats, it will be much easier to stay with the pattern. Fear not. By the time you get halfway through you'll have it memorized and be imagining other uses for this pretty stitch.

When the Wrap has reached the length you prefer, or you run out of yarn, you can either begin the second Edge or bind off and sew on the one you worked at the beginning and put aside.

Alpaca/silk yarn is both warm and light with a delicious feel. One of the advantages to working with a fiber that has silk in it is that it drapes beautifully. ✺

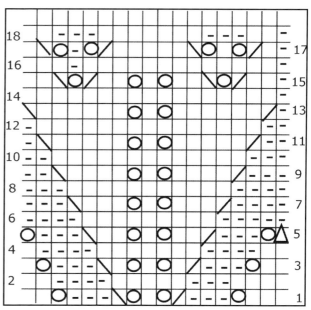

Tulip Lace - Repeat: 18 stitches & 18 rows

Blue Tulip Wrap

The Blue Tulip Wrap is almost exactly the same as the Rose Shearwater Wrap but with a different Lace Pattern for the Main Panel and Moss Stitch Edges. It is larger because it was knit with a worsted weight yarn on #8 needles and used 8 skeins of yarn (110 yds each). The yarn is a very soft, lovely merino wool that is both warm and silky to the touch. I am not overly fond of wool but some of the new merino wools are as soft as alpaca. I bought this because I fell in love with the color.

Both the Blue Tulip Wrap and the Rose Shearwater are best knit with smooth yarns that give good stitch definition which shows off the pattern. Unlike Old Shale and Horseshoe Lace, these patterns tend to get lost when knit with a highly textured yarn. Stitch count is the same as for the Rose Shearwater Wrap:

10+18+18+18+10=74 stitches

Cast on 74 stitches and knit twelve rows in Moss Stitch:

Row 1 (RS): (K1, P1), repeat across
Row 2 (WS): (P1, K1), repeat cross

Note: One of the blessings of the internet is that it has brought the knitters of the world together. However there is one slight issue: Knitters now realize that we do not all share the same conventions, we use different symbols to represent the same stitches, and we also call traditional patterns by different names. I learned early in my knitting life that (RS: K1, P1, WS: P1, K1) was called "Moss Stitch". However, recently I have learned

that in some places that stitch pattern is known as "Seed Stitch". There are two variations on Moss Stitch, the one I learned and this one:

On even number of stitches:

Rows 1(RS) and 2(WS): (K1, P1), repeat across
Rows 3(RS) and 4(WS): (P1, K1), repeat across

For our purposes here, I'll continue to call the first Moss Stitch, but be aware that in different knitting instructions Moss Stitch may mean something different.

On last row place markers:

K10, marker, (K18, marker) 3x

Begin the Edge with Trellis Border on either side and 3 repeats of Tulip Lace (chart above). Like the Shearwater Lace this pattern requires a little bit of shuffling around with the Marker, but it establishes itself after a couple of vertical repeats and you may well be able to work without Markers.

Work until the stole is as long as you like or until you are running out of yarn. Knit twelve rows in Moss Stitch and bind off loosely. **ঙে**

Trudi's Shawl

I knit this shawl for my friend Trudi. It is a luxurious 30" x 72". In a sense this is another variation on the Scrapbag Stole because it is knit with four strands of lace-weight or fingering-weight yarn held together. I was sorting through my stash and discovered these four yarns—leftovers from other projects—that, on their own, would have made a decent-sized scarf, but worked together made a large shawl. The yarns used are a lace-weight silk noil in green, a lace-weight alpaca in sapphire blue, a fine variegated mohair in earthtones, and a fingering-weight sky-blue wool. The pattern is Feather and Fan (chart at right) which is very similar to Old Shale without the "ridge" created by the one WS knit row. The Edge is simply four rows of Garter Stitch and the Borders are 12 stitches in Moss Stitch (RS: K1, P1, WS: P1, K1). As you will discover as you work these Lace Patterns, the same basic design can be adjusted slightly to create many looks.

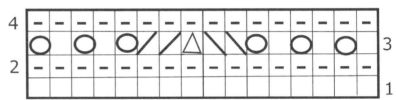

Feather and Fan Lace - Repeat: 16 stitches & 4 rows

The concept of Old Shale, minus the "ridge" and with the addition of 3 stitches knit together instead of RSK2tog and LSK2tog, creates Feather and Fan. Feather and Fan repeated 4 times and then offset by 8 stitches and repeated 4 times creates Ostrich Plume. Varitions are endless for the adventurous Lace knitter! ఇ౮ఞ

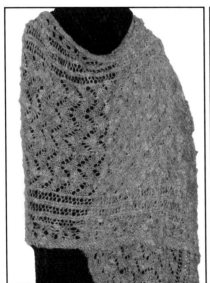

Jane's Stole, on the left, is 32"x 68" and features two Borders. The fiber is a silk and rayon blend in a slubby, recycled fiber purchased from an eBay vendor. The Main Panel is knit in Horseshoe Lace. The Borders are 3 repeats of Insertion Lace and one repeat of Snowdrop Lace. The Traveling Vine Scarf, on the right, is 14" x 64" plus fringe. The yarn is a soft alpaca/silk knit on #6 needles. The Main Panel is Traveling Vine (close-up on page 6.)

The Coveted Scarf

While I was working on this book a new yarn shop called Coveted Yarn (www.covetedyarn.com) opened here in Gloucester. I stopped by and they carry one of my favorite brands of yarn, Blue Heron. In their discount bin I found a 375-yard skein of Blue Heron's Texture in "Lilac" so I decided to knit a "Coveted Scarf". Since I only had the one skein, I wanted to make the most of it. See the tail in the photo below? That's all the yarn I had left when I finished.

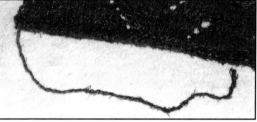

Before beginning to wind the ball, I measured 6 yards of yarn and placed a small, loose slip-knot at the six yard mark. Then I wound as usual. I cast on 36 stitches and worked 6 rows of Garter Stitch. Then place markers after the eleventh stitch and the 25th stitch on the right-side row and knit according to the chart below. Continue to work in pattern until you finish the row closest to the slip-knot. Now start knitting in Garter Stitch until you have one yard left. Use that to bind off and I guarantee you that you won't have much yarn left over! ❧

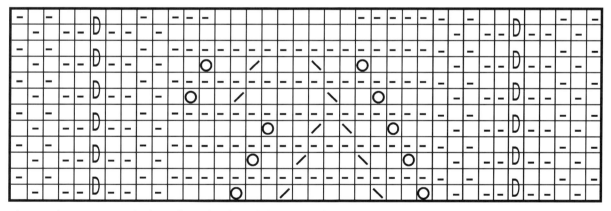

The Coveted Scarf Pattern - The elongated D is the only stitch that is unusual. On WS rows, slip that stitch from the left needle to the right and, at the same time, make a yarn-over, then continue to work in pattern. On the RS row, when you come to that stitch, work the slipped stitch and the YO as one K stitch.

WORKS IN PROGRESS

Once you've tried a few of the projects described in this book—whether you follow my designs or go off on your own—I hope you'll be eager for your own creations. On these pages are a few works-in-progress from my own knitting bag. There are so many good Lace Pattern books available that you could take one Basic Diagram and make endless variations on it. I download Lace charts from the internet all the time. With sites like Ravelry.com, MyPicot.com, Knitty.com, etc. you can build a library of your own Lace at no cost. Barbara G. Walker and Marianne Kinzel have books available that are loaded with tempting Lace Patterns. And the new trend in knitting has produced some amazing designers who offer even more. Annie Modisette, Joan MacGowan-Michael, and Jackie Erickson-Schweitzer are three of my favorite designers who work extensively with Lace.

The fiber for this project is a laceweight alpaca/silk in a dreamy color called, ironically, "Mermaid". I am knitting it on #3 needles and my plan is to make a rectangular shawl using the same layout as Emily's Shawl. I am knitting the Main Panel in Rose Trellis and am planning the Border Lace to be a variation of Marianne Kinzel's Rose Leaf Lace.

I haven't decided on the Edge Lace yet, but I think a Roses theme is definitely worth following. ⮞○⮜

Below left is the two-color silk that I used for the sample on page 30. After experimenting with a number of stitches, I finally picked the Lacey Braid Pattern used in the beige cashmere scarf on page 7. There are three repeats of that pattern separated by an Insertion Lace section with the Slip Stitch used on the Coveted Scarf. That is a nice accent stitch that looks great when used sparingly. The Borders are Trellis Lace and the Edges are the same as those shown on page 30. ⮞○⮜

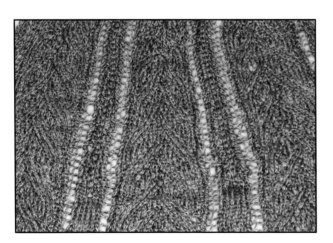

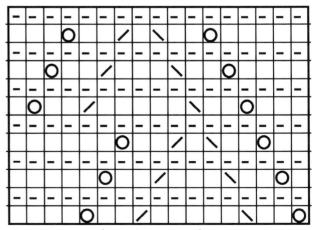

Lacy Braid Lace - Repeat: 17 stitches & 12 rows

This dazzling silver fiber was a surpirse treat from a friend who was cleaning out her stash. It is a cotton/rayon blend with a liquid drape and a shimmery lustre. I am working on #5 needles in a combination of two Lace Patterns - one called Hanging Vine that I downloaded from the internet and the other a simple variation on the Insertion Lace used in the Silk Chenille Stole but with 5 stockinette stitches between each repeat. I call it my Slinky Silver Stole. I plan to crochet a picot edging when it is long enough. ❧

I wish you could see the luster of this yarn. It is a 50% cashmere/ 50% silk blend from an eBay vendor. This one is also going to be a rectangular shawl on the order of Beth's Shawl. The Main Panel is similar to Marianne Kinzel's Arabesque. I haven't decided on the rest. ❧

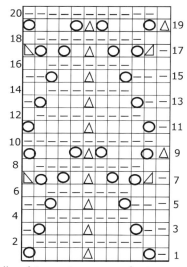

Shells and Stones - Repeat: 12 stitches & 20 rows

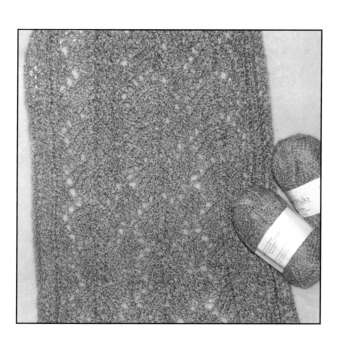

I think my favorite fiber to knit with is Pima cotton. It just feels so good in my hands. This nubby cotton boucle from KnitPicks is one of my very favorite yarns. It is cool in summer, warm in winter, washes beautifully and is extremely soft. I made myself a summer sweater in their "Azure" and had several balls leftover, so decided to knit a scarf. The Border is Trellis Lace, the Edges are Moss Stitch and the Main Panel is one I call Shells and Stones. ❧

The LadyE Cocoon, made from a shawl knit with 3 strands of lace weight yarn, 2 wool and 1 silk on #7 needles

Left, luscious Black Cocoon knit with 2 strands of fingering weight yarn, 1 cashmere and 1 silk on #5 needles

Rose Bouclé Cocoon knit from 100% wool bulky bouclé in stockinette stitch on #11 needles, to give it a lacy look.

THE COCOON:
BY ACCIDENT OR DESIGN

Discovering how to make a cocoon came as a happy accident for me. I had made a long rectangle shawl out of black cashmere and silk. It was beautiful—except for one thing. Nobody ever told me not to knit length-wise instead of width-wise. When I tried to wear it, it stretched uncontrollably. After a lot of tears, I got the idea to transform it into a cocoon. It worked like magic and I applied the technique to two more "mistakes" and loved the results. Next time I might make one on purpose.

Sometimes the best ideas go awry. When that happens with knitting you have a couple of choices—you can rip it out and start over, you can pretend it is something other than it was intended to be and give it to an unsuspecting friend, you can drop it off at the resale shop and hope some ambitious crafter will buy it to take apart and re-knit, or you can get creative. In the case of the Luscious Black Cocoon, getting creative seemed like the best alternative. The fiber was lovely—2 strands of fingering-weight yarn, 1 black cashmere and 1 black silk—and the pattern was pretty, Horseshoe Lace with a Moss Stitch Border. But, despite all that, it proved to be unwearable.

Because I am always experimenting and because I had just purchased a 60" circular needle, I decided to try knitting a rectangular stole lengthwise instead of width-wise. I had decided on Horseshoe Lace for my pattern and I cast on enough stitches to make the stole 74" in length. I knit a few rows of Moss Stitch and then began the Horseshoe Lace. It was both beautiful and fun to work on. When I had knit 17 vertical repeats of the pattern I ended with more Moss Stitch and was eager to wear my new creation—except I immediately realized I had a problem. Because of the direction of the Lace Pattern the shawl just would not behave. It stretched, seemingly endlessly, when I tried to block it and I was faced with owning a stole that could easily be about 20" wide by a hundred or more inches long. I was distraught.

I seriously considered ripping it out and re-knitting the whole thing, but somehow that idea did not appeal to me. I also considered crocheting a non-stretching Border that would more or less force the Lace to stay

where I wanted it but, well, that didn't seem like such a great idea either. My poor shawl languished in limbo while I tried to decide what to do.

It seemed there should be some way to use the unusal direction of stretch to advantage. I'm not really sure what made me decide to try making it into a cocoon but, as soon as I did, it became quite exciting to work on. I folded the piece in half lengthwise, as shown in the diagram on the next page and, allowing 3 inches for the back of the neck, I marked the point where the corners should connect with pieces of colored yarn. Then I opened the piece and laid it flat. Taking Corner A (see Diagram) I folded the stole at a right angle until Corner A met Point A. It took some adjusting to get the width-wise end to fit the lengthwise side and leave a few inches open for the cuff but, of course, the joy of working with knits is that they are somewhat adjustable for these situations. I allowed roughly 8 inches for the cuff area and then used leftover yarn from the project to weave the two edges together to form the shoulder/sleeve seam. I did the same for the other side.

Fortunately I had a good deal of yarn left over from the shawl. When the two seams were finished I used four double-pointed needles to pick up stitches around the opening that I allowed for the cuff. In the photograph on the next page I exaggerated the contrast on the image so you can see the way the cuff is attached to the end of the sleeves. Because the shawl was knit with a Moss Stitch Border, it created a natural band.

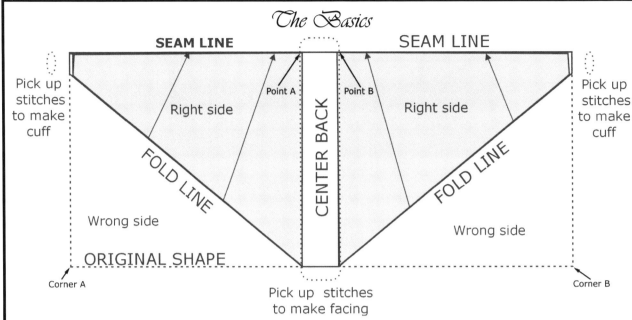

The Basics

SEAM LINE   SEAM LINE

Pick up stitches to make cuff

Point A   Point B

Right side   Right side

CENTER BACK

Point A   Point B

Pick up stitches to make cuff

FOLD LINE   FOLD LINE

Wrong side   Wrong side

ORIGINAL SHAPE

Corner A   Corner B

Pick up stitches to make facing

Cocoons in this section follow this construction. They begin with a rectangular shawl or scarf that has been worked in one piece. Following the above diagram, the short ends of the rectangle are folded up at a 45 degree angle, leaving a space for the cuffs, and stitched in place to form the shoulders. Then, using circular needles or four doublepoint needles for the cuffs, stitches are picked up and a facing and cuffs are knit on.

To create the cuff I picked up 44 stitches, divided them between the 3 needles and worked K2, P2 all the way around.

When both cuffs were complete, I still had a fair amount of yarn left so I decided to crochet around the opening as indicated by dotted lines in the Diagram above. Again the Moss Stitch Border made a nice facing and the addition of the crocheted Lace to give the final

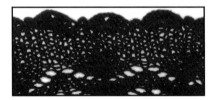

piece a more finished look. I made a simple scalloped edge composed of 5 dbl stitches worked in the same stitch and with a little picot made of 3 sc stitches in between.

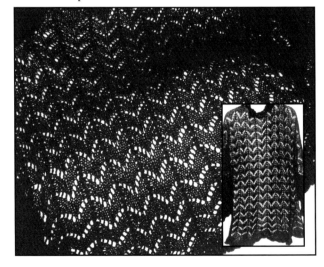

Rose Bouclé Cocoon

The Rose Bouclé Cocoon was another rescue ef-fort that has proven to be a treasure. As I have been writing this book, it is November here in Massachusetts and I have worn that cocoon almost constantly while I work. The yarn was pur-chased from a women's collective in Uruguay that sells hand-painted yarn on the internet. The color, called Barbie

Rose, is one of my favorites, and the yarn is 100% wool in a chunky bouclé with thick-n-thin texture. I decided to knit it on #11 needles to create an open look. I was experimenting with the notion of making a long, rect-angular shawl that was narrower on the two ends than it was in the center back. To accomplish this, I gradually in-creased the number of stitches across the width to add a few inches and then decreased in the same manner for the second half of the shawl. The result was a warm, snuggly wrap that I rarely wore because it felt awkward—I was always dropping it.

Since the Black Cocoon was such a sucess, and I found I was wearing it all the time, I decided to try the same thing with this one. This proved to be an excellent decision because the wider center back allowed the cocoon to drape down gracefully in the back but the shorter ends allowed for sleeves that were not overly long and awkward.

I assembled the cocoon in the same manner as the previous one, but this time, because the sleeves were not as long, I allowed for a larger cuff area. Using a 8" circular #8 needle, I picked up the stitches around the cuff and knit in Garter Stitch until the cuff measured three inches. It is looser than the ribbed cuff on the other cocoon but looks attractive with long-sleeved shirts.

Using a #8 24" circular needle, I then picked up stitches around the opening as indicated by the dotted lines on the chart and did the same thing. The result is a cocoon (shown top left with one of Leslie Wind's pins) that is both practical and elegant. **ഇ൝**

Several years ago when everyone was knitting Lady Eleanor Shawls, I made one in a combination hand-painted wool and silk. However, when it was finished I just never wore it. I decided to try converting it into a cocoon and the results are above left. I used a Czech glass button for the closure with a crocheted loop. Above right is a slinky shawl knit from a slubby rayon yarn in six colors. But, like the Black Cocoon, it has too much vertical stretch. It may well be the next cocoon to join my collection. **ഇ൝**

Aunt Rosie's Rosy Shawl, knit for my godmother, is constructed from a bias knit center panel of Garter Stitches, and an Old Shale Border. It is soft, warm and fits well around the shoulders.

BONUS SECTION:
KNITTING ON THE BIAS

I am including this section for my friend Jan who thinks it is amazing that I knit on the bias. Anyone can and there is a really good reason to do it—it looks more sophisticated than it is and it makes shawls and scarves that have fluid, figure-hugging drape. Plus it is ridiculously easy.

Knitting on the bias can be done in many knit stitches, but the easiest and most attractive is plain old Garter Stitch. This is how you knit on the bias:

Knit with four colors of a soft thick-and-thin wool from HandpaintedYarns.com, this scarf shows-off the diagonal stitch technique. The scarf was made for my friend Leslie Wind whose beautiful hand-made shawl pins are shown in some photos here. See more of her work at www.LeslieWind.com

K all rows. In the last stitch of every right side (RS) row make one (M1) stitch. At the end of every wrong side (WS) row knit 2 stitches together (LSK2tog) to decrease 1.

That's it. To try this, cast on 30 stitches in a worsted-weight yarn on #8 needles (or whatever size you feel comfortable with). Knit a RS row and then a WS row. Knit the second RS row but in the last stitch, M1 stitch by knitting 2 stitches into the last stitch on the needle. Turn and knit the WS but this time decrease (D1) one stitch by knitting the last two stitches together (LSK2tog). Continue in this manner until you can see the bias and get a feel for it. This is all you need to do to create a lot of interesting and attractive scarves but, of course, there are variations that you can try. When you use multiple colors or textures of yarn the effect is more noticeable and more dramatic.

Most of the time you will be satisfied with letting the ends be at an angle as shown in the multi-colored scarf at left and in the Barbie Rose one on the next page, but you can also make square ends. This is better if you plan to add a knit border, like that shown in the Rose Shawl on the facing page.

The photograph on the next page shows a sample of how this is done. Cast on two stitches and proceed according to the following:

K all rows. In the last stitch of each row M1 stitch.

When the piece is as wide as you would like it to be you then change to M1 at the end of RS rows and D1 at the end of WS rows.

Judging the appropriate width of a Bias Knit piece can be a little bit of a challenge. I have torn out

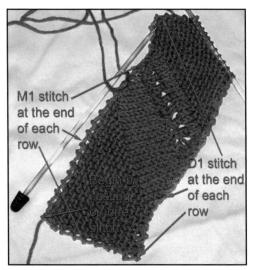

Sample illustrates a swatch knit according to the instructions on the previous page. As you can see the middle section is worked in stockinette stitch with three rows of Eyelette Lace. This was knit in worsted-weight merino wool on #8 needles.

more than a few pieces because, after knitting for several inches, I decided they were narrower than I wanted. Because you are knitting on the bias it may seem that the garment is wide enough. This is a matter of personal taste. Because bias-knit garments stretch more than straight-knit pieces, a little extra width won't be as problematic. The beauty of the drape compensates for it.

Aunt Rosie's Rosy Shawl

The shawl in the photo on page 44 was knit holding together a strand of ultra-soft, rose-colored alpaca and a strand of a slinky pastel-colored rayon yarn on #8 needles. The center panel was knit with a squared beginning and end in Garter Stitch. It is approximately 18" wide and 64" long.

This is another example of adjusting your design when you are not sure how much yarn you have. By knitting the center panel and then a knit-in-the-round Border, you can make the finished piece as large as you would like it to be, if you have more yarn than you need, or finish it when yarn is running out.

For this piece I used a #8 circular needle and picked up stitches around the perimeter, making sure to add a stitch marker at each of the four corners. Work each corner as follows:

Round 1: Before a stitch marker make 1 YO, slip the marker, K1, YO, resume working in pattern. Round 2: Knit in pattern slipping marker as you work. Repeat.

This method creates a tidy mitered corner. Old Shale is one of the "friendliest" stitches for this type of Border because it is formed from four rows, only one of which is a pattern row. It is worked in the round as follows:

Round 1: K all. Round 2: P all. Round 3: K all. Round 4 (pattern row): [(LSK2tog)3x, YO, (K1, YO) 5x, (RSK2tog) 3x, place marker] repeat all the way around.

Continue working those 4 rounds until you are satisfied with the depth of your Border. As additional stitches are added at the four corners knit them in pattern, adding markers as necessary. You can bind off after Rounds 1, 2 or 3.

This is a simple pattern that works up beautifully. It can be worked in a chunky yarn on large needles or a finer yarn on small needles. ❧

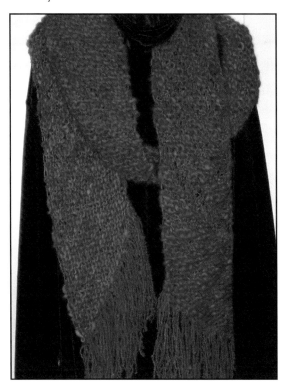

This diagonal scarf was knit from thick-and-thin yarn from HandpaintedYarns.com in "Barbie Rose". It has accent rows and is trimmed with some of the bouclé wool left over from the Rose Cocoon on page 43.

KNITTERLY NOTES

Reading Charts

I find charts to be much more helpful in any sort of pattern knitting than written instructions. Books that offer charted directions usually contain a key to the chart. The one for this book is on page 7. Most charts can be used for both straight knitting (done on straight needles or on a circular needle but knitting back and forth) and for knitting in the round (done on either circular or double-pointed needles.) If you are left-handed, working from charts will probably be much easier for you than working from written directions.

Straight Knitting

When knitting back and forth on straight needles you need to remember that the odd-numbered rows (1, 3, 5, 7, etc.) will always be your right-side (RS) rows. The even-numbered rows are your wrong-side (WS) rows. To knit you read the chart in the directions of the arrows as indicated on the charts below. If the directions (or your own preference) say to make 5 repeats of a pattern then you will work each row of the chart 5 times (placing a stitch marker after each repeat) before turning your piece to start the next row. By adapting to the method outlined on page 13, for RSK2tog and LSK2tog, it is easier for left-handed knitters to adjust their stitches to achieve the desired result.

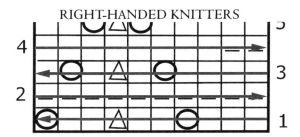 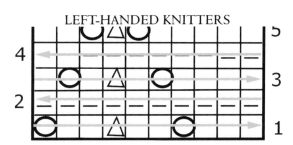

Circular Knitting

When knitting in the round (circular knitting) you will always be knitting in the same direction (right to left for righties, left to right for lefties). It is a good idea to have a different color marker to indicate the beginning of your work. You may also tie a piece of yarn in a contrasting color to indicate your first marker. Both the RS and the WS are worked in the same direction so it is important to remember that even-numbered rows must be worked so the stitch indicated in the chart will be on the <u>WS</u> of the piece. In other words, if the chart indicates purled stitches on the WS, you will *knit* those rows. If an even-number row contains a / or a \ work them as \ and /. I hope this makes sense to you. Once you make the mental adjustment, you will be able to work virtually any charted pattern in the round whether you are right-handed or left-handed. ❧

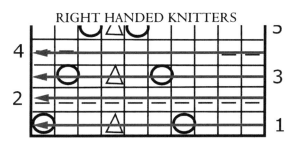 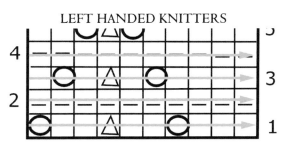

More about / and \...

On page 13 I gave a brief explanation of K2tog and SSK vs. RSK2tog and LSK2tog. Depending on how you learned to knit the loops that form the K stitches of your knitting will either be on your needle facing the left or the right. Once again, because I learned to knit Continental style, my loops have always gone the "wrong"

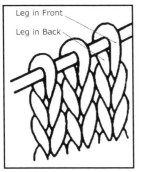

Knit American Style - the "leg" of the stitch is in front of the needle.

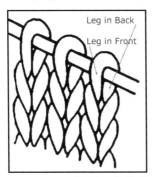

Knit Continental Style - the "leg" of the stitch is in back of the needle.

way. I have also met left-handed knitters who have the "legs" of their loops going the wrong way. You can teach yourself to correct this by just reversing the direction of your wrap on each stitch. That's one way to correct the problem. But I want to tell you something—if you learn a couple of easy tricks it doesn't matter which way your loops go. The finished piece will look the same.

Lace is created in knitting by the placement of YOs that create the little "holes", and stitches knit together to create the curves and ridges that give Lace its beauty.

The image below is an example of a Lace Pattern called "Feather Lace". As you can see, YOs create the lacy holes along either side. Each YO is compensated for by 2 stitches knit together. The RSK2tog on the left form a pretty ridge slanting to the center and the LSK2tog do

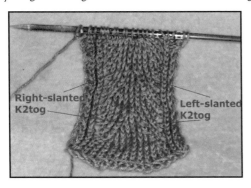

the same on the right. *The important thing to remember, in order to make the slants uniform and neat, is that when 2 stitches are knit together they need to be positioned on the needle so that the stitch which is knit first falls on top of the stitch which is knit second.* In order to get the correct placement of stitches I find it easier to just slip the stitches that are in the wrong orientation off the left-hand needle (or the right-hand needle for lefties)

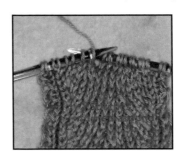

with the tip of the opposite needle, turn them around and slide them back into place and knit them together. As you can see in the photos below this gives you the attractive slant that makes the Lace Pattern so pretty. As long as you remember that, when there are RSK2tog and LSK2tog in any pattern, one set of stitches will be simply knit together and the other set will need to be turned around, it doesn't matter how you wrap your yarn as you work.

In fact, once I got used to doing my K2togs this way I started anticipating the pattern when purling on the WS and would wrap my stitches in the opposite direction for my RSK2togs. That way I didn't have to turn the stitches around when I came to them. I'm not going to ask you to do that but, who knows, you might decide to give it a try.

You can do the same thing when you need to K3tog in either direction. As long as the first stitch your needle goes through is positioned in the proper direction and falls on top of the next stitches the results will be the same. ❧◊❧

Choosing Needles

If you are a veteran knitter you probably have an impressive collection of needles. If you are new to knitting, or new to Lace knitting, you might benefit from a few tips. The most important thing with Lace knitting is a needle with a good, well-tapered point—especially when you are working with a very fine yarn. A sharp tip helps you "dig" in when knitting stitches together.

One of the things that will effect your choice of needle is the type of yarn you are working with. When working with very smooth and/or silky yarns you may benefit from a needle that is not too slick. In my needle collection I have a number of needles that are known as "turbos" for their super-smooth surface. They are wonderful when working with wool and when working with worsted weight yarn or plain knitting. Some time ago I had started a shawl using a fine alpaca/silk yarn and I cast it on my turbos. What a miserable time I had! The yarn slipped all over the place and kept trying to slide off the needles. At first I blamed the yarn but then I tried transferring the piece to bamboo needles and, like magic, the problem was solved. So save your super-slick needles for wool and plain-knitting projects.

Wood and bamboo are excellent for working with fine and "slippy" yarns. They are wonderful when working with silk and with pima cotton. They also warm in your hands as you work. Some bamboo and wooden needles do not have the sharp points you may find you want (Knit-Pick's Harmony line are excellent). When shopping take a good look at the tips and note if they are sharp enough for your needs or too rounded. I purchased a pair of expensive, beautiful ebony needles that had a nice, sharp point but they turned out to be unfortunately fragile. One snapped in two in the midst of a knitting frenzy.

Steel needles have good sharp points and are fairly slick. They are good when working with cashmere, alpaca, and fine merino wool. My only problem with steel needles is that they are inflexible and, since I have arthritis in my hands, can be painful to work with for long periods of time.

Recently I have acquired several pairs of **acrylic** needles which are transparent and come in pretty colors. They have proven to be very pleasant to use. They are lightweight, have good sharp tips, and are pretty. Like steel, they are inflexible but they are fine when working with silk and cotton and are also inexpensive.

My favorite needles for Lace knitting are a soft, special type of **plastic** needle called Bryspun. They are flexible which is wonderful for those of us with arthritic hands. The plastic they are made of provides a little "give" and they warm nicely as you handle them. The points are reasonably sharp. They can be hard to find but I am on a mission to own as many lengths and sizes as I can acquire. Anything that makes it easier to knit for longer periods of time gets my approval. 🙂

Non-Rolling Borders

I've mentioned this other places in the text but if you knit any pattern that is mostly knit on one side and mostly purled on the other side, regardless of YOs and stitches knit together, you will notice that the right and left Borders of your work tend to "roll". If you plan to pick the Borders up and knit around or to add a knitted-on edge Lace this is not a problem but, when knitting scarves and stoles, it is a good idea to add a non-rolling Border to prevent this.

On page 30 I give directions for the Trellis Border which is my favorite Border Lace to avoid rolling but there are many other options. One of the simplest is to knit a Border of five or more stitches in Garter Stitch (K on both RS and WS). Another is to knit a Border of five or more stitches in Moss Stitch or Seed Stitch (see page 35 for more about these stitches). Because they are composed of alternating K and P stitches they'll keep the Border from rolling.

I have also used a backwards rib stitch when I want the Border to be narrow. P1, K1, P1 on the RS and K1, P1, K1 on the WS does an effective job and when worked over 5 stitches (P1, K1, P1, K1, P1) will not roll. Another rather interesting technique is to work reverse stockinette stitch over 5 stitches for either Border and just let it roll—however in the opposite direction of the main panel. This gives an attractive little roll at the edge which is counter to the main panel.

Of course there is no shortage of pretty edge Laces to use, too! 🙂

More Ramblings About Yarn and Where to Buy It

In the chapter on My Process I wrote about yarn but I've been asked to write more about how I choose yarn, where I find it, and other things that you may or may not want to know. Everything here is based on my own experience and other knitters may disagree.

The current knitting revolution has brought many gorgeous, as well as many ugly, yarns to the market. But, of course, one knitter's "ugly" is another knitter's fabulous. For most projects I prefer to work with natural fibers but sometimes I come across a synthetic fiber that is just too much fun to resist. There are a number of super soft, very pretty synthetic yarns that are especially good for making projects for babies and children. Busy mommies often don't have the time for the care required for fine fibers and a good-quality synthetic might be appreciated far more. Some of the novelty yarns are just too cute to resist. But for the most part, I prefer to work in natural fibers. They are generally more comfortable to wear, they hold up better over time, and, in many cases, just get prettier as they are used. I have two handknit Irish wool sweaters that are over 20 years old and they get nicer every time they are cleaned.

ALPACA

Alpaca is one of my favorite fibers. It is soft, very warm, takes dye beautifully for rich, luscious colors, and is pleasant to work with. One note, when knitting Lace with fine alpaca be aware that it tends to look "crumpled" as the Lace tumbles down from the needles. This is just a feature of this fiber that will change after the piece is blocked. Alpaca is not as resilient as wool and, as the garment is used, it may soften and seem to lose its shape but don't let that discourage you from using it. It can be cleaned and re-blocked as needed.

I have a heavy vest I knit from a bulky-weight alpaca that I have been wearing for three winters now. It is so warm I often wear it instead of a jacket and it has acquired that relaxed "old-favorite" look that I love. I'm sure it will give me many more cozy winters.

When knitting with alpaca, be aware that it is not as tightly spun as wool so it is easy to split the fiber as you knit. Once aware of this you will adjust easily.

Suri alpaca comes from a special breed of alpaca. The yarn is lustrous and resembles mohair but is much softer without the "prickle" that mohair often has. It is warm and elegant.

CASHMERE

Cashmere is delicious and warm. It is also expensive but, if you are a budget-conscious knitter, there are plenty of options. A small amount of cashmere blended with alpaca or merino can feel as soft and warm as pure cashmere. I have purchased 100% cashmere from several online vendors and been pleased with it. ColourmartUK in England sells nice cashmere in a variety of weights at decent prices. One thing to remember with their yarns is that they are coated for manufacturers who weave with them. This coating will dissolve with the proper washing and the yarn "blooms" quite nicely so don't be surprised if your new cashmere does not feel like cashmere. The Black Cashmere Cocoon was knit from their cashmere and seems to get softer and fluffier the more I wear it.

Knitter's Addiction in Australia is one source for very soft cashmere that is not coated. I recently purchased three 1000-yard balls of 100% cashmere in laceweight. Even with shipping the exchange rate came to a little over $20 per ball. Their colors are lovely.

I have also purchased merino/cashmere blends which are attractive and soft—and much less expensive. One of my favorite fibers is 50% silk/50% cashmere. It has the softness and warmth of cashmere and the lustre and drape of silk. I've purchased it from eBay vendors and also when I could find it in yarn stores. I always find it a pleasure to work with. As mentioned in an earlier chapter, there are online vendors who sell recycled cashmere that they unravel from designer sweaters bought in thrift stores and clean. Usually this yarn is crimpy but it is also extremely soft. The price can be excellent and if you can find 2 or 3 compatible colors you can create stunning garments for a fraction of the price of retail cashmere.

COTTON, especially Pima

Cotton is not as elastic as animal fiber so when you first start working with it you have to learn to relax your hold and knit a little looser. Cotton is great for summer wear or in mild climates and is ideal for camisoles and most Lace knitting.

Pima cotton was developed in the American southwest to compete with Egyptian cotton. It is extremely silky and absorbent, takes color well, and comes in a variety of textures. My favorite Pima cotton comes from KnitPicks. I love both their Shine, which is smooth and has superb stitch definition, and their Crayon which is more of a bouclé. I have knit sweaters, bed jackets, scarves, camisoles, and baby garments from Pima cotton and always been pleased with the results. It washes well, is delightful to handle and makes an excellent alternative when knitting for people who are sensitive to animal fibers or who are vegan.

Because cotton is not elastic it tends to lose shape but usually shrinks slightly when washed. If you are going to knit ribbing it is best to carry-along a fine elastic.

SILK, including Recycled

Silk is my favorite fiber. A small amount of silk blended with alpaca, merino, cotton, or cashmere adds lustre and drape. Silk by itself is elegant. Like cotton it is not elastic and will require a fine carry-along of elastic when knit into ribbing. It is ideal for camisoles and other dainty treats. A little headband or ruff knit of silk can make an elegant and easy gift. I've recently knit a couple pairs of Lace gloves in a silk/merino blend which are just beautiful and so luxurious. No fiber takes dye quite like silk.

ColourmartUK sells wonderful silk and they will wind as many plys on a cone as you want. Blue Heron makes some of the prettiest hand-painted silk yarns in extraordinary colorways. Yarntopia Treasures is another source for exceptional hand-painted yarn. I am currently knitting lace gloves from their silk/wool.

Silk may well be the queen of recycled fibers. As mentioned on page 4, recycled Himilayan silk has become very popular and has the added benefit of providing economic support for people in impoverished areas of the world. There are a few things to be aware of when using recycled silk. First of all, the quality of the yarn varies greatly. Thickness can be inconsistent, however, silk by its very nature is quite strong so even thin sections of the yarn are usually strong. You may also find bits of twigs and leaves in your yarn. I just pluck them out and remind myself that those twigs came from halfway around the world. Second, the spinning is often inconsistent. Some of the yarn I have purchased has been spun so tightly that the yarn curls up as I wind the balls. My solution to this is to stick a double-pointed needle through the ball, secure the yarn around it and just drop the ball, holding onto about a yard of the yarn, and let it spin—sort of the opposite of drop-spindle spinning. When the ball starts to spin slowly I wrap the length of yarn onto the ball, secure it and drop the next yard. This relaxes the spin enough to make the yarn more pliant.

I knit the Gypsy Shawl out of 10 skeins of Himalayan silk. Once I washed it I was astonished at how soft it became. It is one of my all time favorite projects.

Some years ago I purchased 2 cones of yarn in a shop in Puerto Plata, Dominican Republic that was called Haitian Silk. It is a thick-thin yarn with lots of slubs that are lustrous. I believe the yarn is more rayon than silk but it has a nice hand and the colors are soft and pretty.

Banana Silk is another popular recycled yarn. It is actually closer to rayon than silk because it is manufactured from the fibers of banana plants. Most banana silk is handspun from scraps left from clothing manufacturing. It is extremely shiny and, like rayon, a bit stiff but softens with washing. Like recycled silk the spinning can be inconsistent and the drop-spindle "un-spinning" method works well with it. It is nice for use with recycled silk.

I have also purchased silk unraveled from silk sweaters on eBay. The Silk Roving Stole is my only adventure in unraveling a sweater and knitting with it but I will definitely try that again if I ever find anything comparable to that amazing garment.

ANGORA & MOHAIR

Emily's Shawl is knit from a lovely merino/angora blend. The yarn used in Rebecca's Shawl (the second Mermaid Shawl) is a rayon/angora blend from Webs and it is a beautiful yarn to work with. It adds softness and warmth and that feel of luxury. I find angora spun with a small amount of nylon is sturdier and easier to knit with no loss of softness and bloom.

The Violet Sampler Shawl is knit from Ironstone Mohair and a strand of silk to add drape. Ironstone mohair has a beautiful lustre and is softer than other mohairs I have worked with. Brown Sheep makes a wonderful wool/mohair blend that is available in worsted weight for warm shawls and scarves. Rowan's Kid Silk Haze is one of the loveliest mohairs available. ❧

Kathleen Valentine is a novelist who also happens to knit. Her novel, **The Old Mermaid's Tale** was the original inspiration for this book's title shawl. She is also the author of **My Last Romance and other passions** and **Each Angel Burns**, a novel to be published in 2009. Her web sites include www.MermaidShawl.com, www.KathleenValentine.com, her blog at www.ParlezMoiBlog.blogspot.com, and a new venture, an e-press at www.HeartThrobBooks.com. She is working on a second knitting book which will feature lace bed jackets, camisoles and accessories. You can find her on Ravelry as KathleenV. Her professional web site is www.Valentine-Design.com.

A Few Words About the Photography

Gloucester, Massachusetts, where I live and knit, is located at the tip of Cape Ann forty miles north of Boston. It is the oldest fishing community in America and is, as I always say, my hometown of choice. The photographs of the garments in this book were mostly shot in Gloucester. Locations include The Hammond Estate, Montgomery's Boatyard, Briar Neck overlooking Thacher Island with its twin stone lighthouses, and The Charles Hovey House overlooking Ten Pound Island with its white lighthouse. The appearance of the Schooner Thomas E. Lannon (www.Schooner.org) in some of these pictures was a happy accident on the day we were shooting. Throughout the book I have added photographs of Gloucester by my friend, photographer Jay Albert. His photographs of the lobster boats, sailing ships, and local scenery can be found on his blog at www.CapeAnnImages.blogspot.com.

I am especially indebted to my lovely friends who modeled for me; Jane Daniel, Clare Higgins, Rebecca Reynolds, and Constance Rohrbough; my sister, Beth Valentine Pelligrini; and my niece, Emily Beimel. Some of the shawls are shown with shawl pins created by Leslie Wind, www.LeslieWind.com.